GW00567367

KitchenAid®

Recipe Collection

Publications International, Ltd.

Copyright © 2014 Publications International, Ltd.
All rights reserved. This publication may not be reproduced or quoted in whole or in part by any means whatsoever without written permission from:

Louis Weber, CEO
Publications International, Ltd.
7373 North Cicero Avenue
Lincolnwood, IL 60712

Permission is never granted for commercial purposes.

Recipes and text on pages 18, 21, 37, 48, 53, 54, 60, 63, 76, 78, 85, 118, 121, 123, 154, 168, 260, 264, 270, 277, 278, 237, 241, 242, 243, 244, 288, 289, 290, 293, 300, 304 and 310 copyright © 2014 KitchenAid. All other recipes and text copyright © 2014 Publications International, Ltd. Stand mixer photo on front cover and photos on pages 4–11 copyright © 2014 KitchenAid. All recipe photos copyright © 2014 Publications International, Ltd.

® Registered Trademark/™ Trademark/the shape of the stand mixer is a registered trademark of KitchenAid, U.S.A. © 2014 All rights reserved.

www.KitchenAid.com

Pictured on the front cover *(left to right, top to bottom):* Pots de Crème au Chocolat *(page 300),* Cranberry Chocolate Chunk Muffins *(page 41),* Mini Carnitas Tacos *(page 90),* Carrot Cake *(page 270),* Crusty Pizza Dough *(page 63),* Quick Pasta Puttanesca *(page 112),* Glazed Cornish Hens *(page 170)* and Zesty Zucchini-Chickpea Salad *(page 221).*

Pictured on the back cover *(left to right, top to bottom):* Coconut Scones with Orange Butter *(page 44),* Chocolate Crème Brûlée *(page 298),* Cherry-Lemon Poppy Seed Muffins *(page 34),* Italian Country-Style Braised Chicken *(page 163),* Grilled Strip Steaks with Fresh Chimichurri *(page 132),* Onion and White Bean Spread *(page 80),* White Chocolate Cake *(page 266),* Tortilla Soup *(page 103)* and Cedar Plank Salmon with Grilled Citrus Mango *(page 178).*

ISBN: 978-1-4508-7785-5

Library of Congress Control Number: 2014936298

Manufactured in China.

8 7 6 5 4 3 2 1

Microwave Cooking: Microwave ovens vary in wattage. Use the cooking times as guidelines and check for doneness

Table of **Contents**

glossary of
cooking terms

AL DENTE: The literal translation of this Italian phrase is "to the tooth." It indicates a degree of doneness when cooking pasta. Al dente pasta is slightly firm and chewy, rather than soft.

BASTE: Basting is the technique of brushing, spooning, or pouring liquids over food—usually meat and poultry—as it cooks. Basting helps preserve moistness, adds flavor, and gives foods an attractive appearance. Melted butter, pan drippings, broth, or a combination of these ingredients are frequently used. Sometimes seasonings or flavorings are added.

Beat

BEAT: Beating is the technique of stirring or mixing vigorously. Beating introduces air into egg whites, egg yolks, and whipping cream; mixes two or more ingredients to form a homogeneous mixture; or makes a mixture smoother, lighter, and creamier. Beating can be done with a variety of tools, including a spoon, fork, wire whisk, rotary eggbeater, or electric mixer.

BLANCH: Blanching means cooking foods, most often vegetables, briefly in boiling water and then quickly cooling them in cold water. Food is blanched for one or more of the following reasons: to loosen and remove skin (tomatoes, peaches, almonds); to enhance color and reduce bitterness (raw vegetables for crudités); and to extend storage life (raw vegetables to be frozen).

BLEND: Blending is the technique of mixing together two or more ingredients until they are thoroughly combined. The ingredients may be blended together with an electric mixer or electric blender, or by hand using a wooden spoon or wire whisk.

BOIL: To bring to a boil means to heat a liquid until bubbles break the surface. Boiling refers to cooking food in boiling water. For a "full rolling boil," bubbles break the surface continuously and cannot be stirred away.

KitchenAid

BRAISE: Braising is a moist-heat cooking method used to tenderize tough cuts of meat or fibrous vegetables. Food is first browned in fat and then gently simmered in a small amount of liquid in a tightly covered skillet until tender. This can be done on the rangetop or in the oven. The liquid—such as water, broth, wine, or beer—often has finely chopped vegetables and herbs added for flavor.

BROIL: Broiling is the technique of cooking foods a measured distance from a direct source of heat. Both gas and electric ovens provide a means of broiling. Some rangetops have built-in grills that provide another broiling option. Grilling on a barbecue grill also fits this broad definition of broiling. The goal of broiling is to brown the exterior without overcooking the interior. Generally, the thinner the food item, the closer it should be to the heat source.

BRUSH: Brushing refers to the technique of applying a liquid such as melted butter, barbecue sauce, or glaze to the surface of food prior to or during cooking with a brush. It serves the same purpose as basting: preserving moistness, adding flavor, and giving foods an attractive appearance.

Brush

CARAMELIZE: Caramelizing is the technique of cooking sugar, sometimes with a small amount of water, to a very high temperature (between 310°F and 360°F) so that it melts into a clear brown liquid and develops a characteristic flavor. The color can vary from light golden brown to dark brown. Caramelized sugar, sometimes called "burnt sugar," is used in a variety of desserts and sauces.

CHILL: Chilling is the technique of cooling foods, usually in the refrigerator or over ice, to a temperature of 35°F to 40°F. A recipe or dish may require several hours or as long as overnight to chill thoroughly. To chill a large portion of a hot mixture such as soup or chili, separate the mixture into several small containers for quicker cooling. To chill small amounts of hot food, place the food in a bowl or saucepan over a container of crushed ice or iced water, or chill the food in the freezer for 20 to 30 minutes.

CHOP: Chopping is the technique of cutting food into small, irregularly shaped pieces. Although the term does not designate a specific size, most cooks would suggest that food be chopped into approximately ¼-inch pieces. Chopped food is larger than minced food and more irregularly cut than diced food. Recipe directions may call for a coarsely chopped or a finely chopped ingredient.

Chop

COAT: To coat means to cover food with an outer layer, usually fine or powdery, using ingredients such as flour, crumbs, cornmeal, or sugar. With foods such as chicken, fish fillets, and eggplant, this coating is preliminary to frying or baking and provides a crispy exterior. Such foods are often first rolled in eggs or milk so the coating adheres. Some cookies are coated with sugar before or after baking.

COMBINE: Combining is the process of mixing two or more liquid or dry ingredients together to make them a uniform mixture.

Combine

CORE: Coring means to remove the center seed-bearing structure of a fruit or vegetable. The most commonly cored foods are apples, pears, pineapple, zucchini, and cucumbers. First cutting the food into quarters and then cutting out the center core can accomplish coring with a small knife. A utensil specially designed to remove the core of specific whole fruits and vegetables is known as a corer. The most common corers are for apples, pears, and pineapple.

CREAM: Creaming is the process of softening sugar and butter until the mixture is light or pale in color and well blended. Creaming can be done with a variety of baking tools including a wooden spoon, an electric mixer, or a food processor.

CRIMP: To crimp means to seal two layers of dough together. This process can be done with one's fingertips or a fork, and the term is most commonly used in reference to pie crusts. Depending upon the style of pie, crimping can be used as a decorative finish for ornate desserts.

Crimp

CRUMBLE: To crumble means to break food into small pieces of irregular size. It is usually done with the fingers. Ingredients often crumbled include blue cheese and bacon. Both foods can be purchased in the supermarket already crumbled.

CRUSH: Crushing means reducing a food, such as crackers, to small fine particles by rolling with a rolling pin or pounding with a mortar and pestle. A food processor or blender also works well. Fruit can be crushed to extract its juices. Garlic is sometimes crushed with the flat side of a knife blade or garlic press to release its flavor.

KitchenAid

CUTTING IN: Cutting in is the technique used to combine a chilled solid fat such as shortening or butter with dry ingredients such as flour, so that the resulting mixture is in coarse, small pieces. A fork, two table knives, fingers, or a pastry blender may be used. If using a food processor, be careful not to overmix the ingredients. This process is used to make biscuits, scones, pie pastry, and some cookies.

Cutting In

DEGLAZE: Deglazing is the technique used to retrieve the flavorful bits that adhere to a pan after a food, usually meat, has been browned and the excess fat has been drained. While the pan is still hot, a small amount of liquid (water, wine, or broth) is added and stirred to loosen the browned bits in the pan. The resulting liquid is used as a base for sauces and gravies.

DEGREASE: Degreasing is a technique used to remove fat from the surface of a liquid such as soup or broth. It can be accomplished in several ways. First remove the soup or broth from the heat and allow it to stand briefly until the fat rises. The quickest degreasing method is to skim off the fat using a large spoon. If the fat to be removed is animal fat, the liquid may be chilled; the animal fat will harden, making it easy to lift off.

DICE: To dice is to cut food into small cubes that are uniform in size. The smallest dice, which is about ⅛ of an inch, is best suited for delicate garnishing. More typical are sizes between ¼ and ½ of an inch. Dicing is distinguished from chopping and mincing by the care taken to achieve a uniform size for an attractive presentation.

DOT: This term, generally used in cooking as "to dot with butter," refers to cutting butter into small bits and scattering them over a food. This technique allows the butter to melt evenly. It also keeps the food moist, adds richness, and can promote browning.

DUST: Dusting is a technique used to lightly coat a food, before or after cooking, with a powdery ingredient such as flour or powdered sugar. The ingredient may be sprinkled on using your fingers or shaken from a small sieve or a container with holes on the top. A greased baking pan can be dusted with flour before it is filled, a technique also known as "flouring."

FLAKE: To flake refers to the technique of separating or breaking off small pieces or layers of a food using a utensil, such as a fork. For example, cooked fish fillets may be flaked for use in a salad or main dish.

FLOUR: To flour means to apply a light coating of flour to a food or piece of equipment. Applied to food, the flour dries the surface. This helps food brown better when frying and keeps food such as raisins from sticking together. Baking pans are floured for better release characteristics and to produce thin, crisp crusts. Rolling pins, biscuit cutters, cookie cutters, and work surfaces are floured to prevent doughs from sticking to them.

FOLD: Folding is a specialized technique for combining two ingredients or mixtures, one of which usually has been aerated, such as whipped cream or egg whites. It is best done by placing the airy mixture on top of the other and, with a rubber spatula, gently but quickly cutting through to the bottom and turning the ingredients over with a rolling motion. The bowl is rotated a quarter-turn each time and the process repeated until the mixtures are combined with as little loss in volume as possible. Care must be taken not to stir, beat, or overmix. Fruit pieces, chips, or nuts may be folded into an airy mixture using the same technique.

FRY: Frying refers to the technique of cooking foods in hot fat, usually vegetable oil. Proper fat temperature is critical to a successful result. The ideal temperature produces a crisp exterior and a moist, perfectly cooked interior; too high a temperature will burn the food, and too low a temperature will result in food absorbing excessive fat. A deep-fat thermometer is essential to determining the temperature of the fat. Deep-fried foods are submerged or floated in hot fat in a large heavy saucepan or Dutch oven. Electric deep fryers fitted with wire baskets are available. Pan-frying refers to cooking food in a skillet in a small amount of fat that does not cover the food.

Grate

GLAZE: To glaze a dessert means to add a type of icing or topping that will give the dessert a smooth or shiny finishing coat. There are a number of different types of glazes. Pastry glazes, which are brushed onto dough before baking, are often made of egg, milk, and cream. Caramel and sieved jam can also be used as glazes.

GRATE: Grating refers to the technique of making very small particles from a firm food like carrots, lemon peel, or Parmesan cheese by rubbing it along a coarse surface with small, sharp protrusions, usually a metal kitchen grater. Food may also be grated in a food processor using a specialized metal blade.

KitchenAid

GREASE: To grease a pan means to coat the inside surface of a pan or dish with a layer of fat. Butter, oil, and shortening are the most popular ingredients used for greasing, but recipes will often specify which type of fat to use. Pans can be greased using either a brush or kitchen paper.

KNEAD: Kneading refers to the technique of manipulating bread dough in order to develop the protein in flour, called gluten, to ensure the structure of the finished product. Kneading also aids in combining the dough ingredients. Biscuit dough is lightly kneaded—only about ten times—whereas yeast doughs may be vigorously kneaded for several minutes.

LEVEL: Leveling refers to removing the crown, or rounded part, of a cake to create a flat surface conducive to frosting or decorating. The best way to level a cake is with a sharp serrated knife or a tool called a cake leveler.

MASH: To mash is to crush a food into a soft, smooth mixture, as in mashed potatoes or bananas. It can be done with a tool called a potato masher or with an electric mixer. Small amounts of food, such as one or two bananas or a few hard-cooked egg yolks, can be mashed with a fork. For best results with potatoes, make sure they are fully cooked so they are soft enough to become completely smooth.

Mash

MINCE: Mincing refers to the technique of chopping food into very tiny, irregular pieces. Minced food is smaller than chopped food. Flavorful seasonings, such as garlic and fresh herbs, are often minced to distribute their flavor more evenly throughout a dish.

PURÉE: To purée means to mash or strain a soft or cooked food until it has a smooth consistency. This can be done with a food processor, sieve, blender, or food mill. For best results, the food must be naturally soft, such as raspberries or ripe pears, or cooked until it is completely tender. Puréed foods are used as sauces and as ingredients in other sweet or savory dishes. The term also refers to the foods that result from the process.

PROOF: Proofing is the process by which dough expands and rises, and it is called for in all yeast bread recipes. Dough proofs when it sits in a warm spot, free from draft, for several hours. The dough rises during the proofing process because the yeast ferments, which produces carbon dioxide.

REDUCE: To reduce is to boil a liquid, usually a sauce, until its volume has been decreased through evaporation. This results in a more intense flavor and thicker consistency. Typically, reduced sauces are one third or one half of their original volume. Use a pan with a wide bottom to shorten preparation time. The reduced product is referred to as a "reduction." Since the flavor of any seasonings would also become concentrated when a sauce is reduced, add the seasonings to the sauce after it has been reduced.

ROAST: Roasting involves cooking poultry and large tender cuts of meat in the oven in an uncovered pan. Roasting produces a nicely browned exterior and a moist interior. Roasting vegetables intensifies their natural sweetness. Vegetables such as onions and carrots can be roasted alongside meat. Many vegetables can be roasted and served as a side dish or used as ingredients in other dishes.

Roll Out

ROLL OUT: To roll out means to flatten dough into an even layer using a rolling pin. To roll out pastry or cookie dough, place the dough—which should be in the shape of a disc—on a floured surface, such as a counter, pastry cloth, or a large cutting board. Lightly flour your hands and the rolling pin. Place the rolling pin across the center of the dough. With several light strokes, roll the rolling pin away from you toward the edge of the dough. Turn the dough a quarter-turn and roll again from the center to the edge. Repeat this process until the dough is the desired thickness. If the dough becomes sticky, dust it and the rolling pin with flour. If the dough sticks to the surface, gently fold back the edge of the dough and dust the surface underneath the dough with flour.

Sauté

SAUTÉ: Sautéing is the technique of rapidly cooking or browning food in a small amount of fat in a skillet or sauté pan. The food is constantly stirred, turned, or tossed to keep it from sticking or burning. Thin, tender cuts of meat—such as steaks, lamb chops, sliced pork tenderloin, flattened chicken breasts, and fish fillets—are candidates for sautéing. The objective is to brown the food on the outside in the time needed to cook the interior. This requires medium-high heat. Oil can withstand the higher heat needed for sautéing. For flavor, a little butter can be added to the oil, but do not use only butter because it will burn before the food browns.

SCALD: To scald means to heat some type of liquid, usually a dairy product such as cream, in a saucepan until it is almost boiling. Tiny bubbles around the perimeter of the pan are often a good indicator that the liquid has reached the scalding stage. Scalded milk is often essential to custards, pudding, and sauce recipes.

KitchenAid

SIFT: Sifting is the technique of passing a dry ingredient such as flour or powdered sugar through the fine mesh of a sieve or sifter for the purpose of breaking up lumps and making it lighter in texture. Sifting results in lighter baked goods and smoother frostings. Most all-purpose flour is presifted, but many bakers sift even presifted flour to achieve a fine, light texture. Cake flour is generally sifted before using. Spoon the ingredient into the sieve and push it through the mesh screen using a metal spoon or rubber spatula.

SIMMER: To simmer is to cook a liquid or a food in a liquid with gentle heat just below the boiling point. Small bubbles slowly rising to the surface of the liquid indicate simmering.

Sift

SLIVER: To sliver is the technique of cutting food into thin strips or pieces. Basil and garlic are two ingredients that may be identified as slivered in a recipe.

STEAM: Steaming is a method of cooking food, usually vegetables, in the steam given off by boiling water. The food is held above, but not in, the boiling or simmering water in a covered pan. The steam swirls around the food and cooks it with an intense, moist heat. Steaming helps to retain flavor, color, shape, texture, and many of the vitamins and minerals. Steaming is often done in a two-pan steamer, a steamer basket, or a bamboo steamer.

STRAIN: Straining refers to the technique of pouring a liquid through the small holes of a strainer or the wire mesh of a sieve to remove lumps or unwanted particles.

Whisk

TOAST: Toasting is the technique of browning foods by means of dry heat. Bread products, nuts, seeds, and coconut are commonly toasted. Toasting is done in a toaster, toaster oven, oven, or skillet, or under the broiler. The purpose of toasting bread is to brown, crisp, and dry it. Nuts, seeds, and coconut are toasted to intensify their flavor.

WHIP: To whip refers to the technique of beating ingredients such as egg whites and whipping cream with a wire whisk or electric mixer in order to incorporate air and increase their volume. This results in a light, fluffy texture.

WHISK: Whisking is the technique of stirring, beating, or whipping foods with a wire whisk. If you do not have a whisk, you can use a wooden spoon if the purpose is to blend ingredients. For whipping foods, an electric mixer can be used instead.

breakfast and brunch

Oatmeal Brûlée with Raspberry Sauce

• • •

OATMEAL BRÛLÉE

4 cups water

½ teaspoon salt

3 cups old-fashioned oats

¼ cup granulated sugar

1 cup heavy cream

3 egg yolks

½ teaspoon vanilla

2 tablespoons packed brown sugar

RASPBERRY SAUCE

6 ounces frozen sweetened raspberries

½ cup granulated sugar

¼ cup water

1 teaspoon orange extract

MAKES 4 SERVINGS

1 For brûlée, preheat oven to 300°F. Line baking sheet with foil. Bring 4 cups water and salt to a simmer in medium saucepan over high heat; stir in oats. Reduce heat to low; cook 3 to 5 minutes or until water is absorbed and oats are tender, stirring occasionally. Divide oatmeal among four large ramekins or ovenproof bowls. Place on prepared baking sheet.

2 Whisk egg yolks and ¼ cup granulated sugar in small bowl. Heat cream in small saucepan over high heat until bubbles form around edge; do not boil. Remove from heat; stir in vanilla. Whisking constantly, pour ½ cup hot cream in thin stream into egg mixture. Whisk egg mixture into remaining hot cream mixture in saucepan. Pour cream mixture evenly over oatmeal in ramekins.

3 Bake 35 minutes or until nearly set. Remove from oven; preheat broiler to 500°F. Sprinkle 1½ teaspoons brown sugar evenly over each brûlée. Place baking sheet under broiler; broil 3 to 5 minutes or until tops are caramelized. Cool 5 to 10 minutes before serving.

4 Meanwhile for sauce, combine raspberries, ½ cup granulated sugar, ¼ cup water and orange extract in blender or food processor; blend until puréed. Strain mixture through fine-mesh sieve to remove seeds. Serve with oatmeal brûlée.

KitchenAid

Cornmeal **Pancakes**

• • •

2 cups buttermilk

2 eggs

¼ cup sugar

2 tablespoons butter, melted

1½ cups yellow cornmeal

¾ cup plus 2 teaspoons all-purpose flour, divided

1½ teaspoons baking powder

1 teaspoon salt

1 cup frozen blueberries, thawed

MAKES 4 SERVINGS

1 Whisk buttermilk, eggs, sugar and butter in large bowl until well blended. Combine cornmeal, ¾ cup flour, baking powder and salt in medium bowl; stir into buttermilk mixture. Let stand 5 minutes. Toss blueberries with 2 teaspoons flour.

2 Lightly grease griddle or large skillet; heat over medium heat. Pour about ⅓ cup batter onto hot griddle for each pancake; sprinkle blueberries over batter. Cook about 3 minutes or until tops of pancakes are bubbly and appear dry; turn and cook about 2 minutes or until bottoms are golden.

KitchenAid

Bacon and Egg Cups

• • •

12 slices bacon, cut crosswise into thirds

6 eggs

½ cup diced green bell pepper

½ cup (2 ounces) shredded pepper jack cheese

½ cup half-and-half

¼ teaspoon salt

¼ teaspoon freshly ground black pepper

MAKES 12 SERVINGS

1 Preheat oven to 350°F. Lightly spray 12 standard (2½-inch) muffin pan cups with nonstick cooking spray.

2 Arrange bacon slices in single layer without overlapping on paper towel-lined microwavable plate. Top with additional paper towels. Microwave on HIGH 2 to 3 minutes or until bacon is cooked yet pliable. Place three bacon slices in each cup, overlapping in bottom.

3 Whisk eggs, bell pepper, cheese, half-and-half, salt and black pepper in medium bowl until well blended. Fill each muffin cup with ¼ cup egg mixture. Bake 20 to 25 minutes or until eggs are set in center. Run knife around edge of each cup to loosen; carefully remove from pan. Serve warm.

Peach Pecan Upside-Down Pancake

• • •

2 tablespoons butter, melted

2 tablespoons packed brown sugar

1 tablespoon maple syrup, plus additional for serving

½ (16-ounce) package frozen unsweetened peach slices, thawed

3 tablespoons pecan pieces

⅔ cup biscuit baking mix

2 eggs

⅓ cup milk

½ teaspoon vanilla

MAKES 6 SERVINGS

1 Preheat oven to 400°F. Spray 9-inch pie plate with nonstick cooking spray.

2 Pour butter into prepared pie plate. Sprinkle with brown sugar and drizzle with 1 tablespoon maple syrup. Arrange peach slices in single layer over syrup. Sprinkle with pecans.

3 Place baking mix in medium bowl. Whisk eggs, milk and vanilla in small bowl; stir into baking mix just until moistened. Pour batter over peaches.

4 Bake 15 to 18 minutes or until lightly browned and toothpick inserted into center comes out clean. Cool in pie plate 1 minute. Run knife around edge of pancake; invert onto serving plate. Cut into wedges. Serve immediately with additional maple syrup, if desired.

KitchenAid

Crustless **Ham and Asparagus Quiche**

• • •

2 cups sliced asparagus
(½-inch pieces)

1 red bell pepper,
cut into ¼-inch dice

1 cup milk

2 tablespoons all-purpose flour

4 egg whites

1 egg

1 cup chopped cooked deli ham,
cut into ¼-inch dice

2 tablespoons chopped fresh
tarragon or basil

½ teaspoon salt

¼ teaspoon freshly ground black pepper

½ cup (2 ounces) shredded
Swiss cheese

MAKES 6 SERVINGS

1 Preheat oven to 350°F. Spray 9-inch pie plate with nonstick cooking spray.

2 Combine asparagus, bell pepper and 1 tablespoon water in microwavable bowl. Cover with waxed paper; microwave on HIGH 2 minutes or until vegetables are crisp-tender. Drain.

3 Whisk milk and flour in large bowl. Whisk in egg whites and egg until well blended. Stir in vegetables, ham, tarragon, salt and black pepper. Pour into prepared pie plate.

4 Bake 35 minutes. Sprinkle cheese over quiche; bake 5 minutes or until center is set and cheese is melted. Let stand 5 minutes before serving. Cut into wedges.

VARIATION: Add 1 clove minced garlic and 2 tablespoons chopped green onion for extra flavor.

Oatmeal Pecan **Pancakes**

• • •

1¼ to 1½ cups milk, divided

½ cup old-fashioned oats

⅔ cup all-purpose flour

⅓ cup whole wheat flour

2½ tablespoons packed brown sugar

2 teaspoons baking powder

½ teaspoon baking soda

¼ teaspoon salt

1 egg

2 tablespoons butter, melted

½ cup chopped toasted pecans

Maple syrup

MAKES 4 SERVINGS

1 Bring ½ cup milk to a simmer in small saucepan. Stir in oats. Remove from heat; let stand 10 minutes.

2 Combine all-purpose flour, whole wheat flour, brown sugar, baking powder, baking soda and salt in large bowl; mix well.

3 Combine egg and melted butter in medium bowl; mix well. Stir in oatmeal mixture and remaining ¾ cup milk. Add flour mixture; stir just until blended. If mixture is too thick, add remaining ¼ cup milk, 1 tablespoon at a time. Stir in pecans.

4 Lightly grease large skillet or griddle; heat over medium heat. Drop batter by ¼ cupfuls into skillet; flatten batter slightly. Cook 2 minutes or until tops are bubbly and bottoms are golden brown. Turn and cook until golden brown. Serve immediately with maple syrup.

Bourbon Street **Beignets**

● ● ●

1 package (¼ ounce) active dry yeast

¼ cup warm water (105°F to 115°F)

¼ cup granulated sugar

2 tablespoons shortening

½ teaspoon salt

½ cup boiling water

4 to 4½ cups all-purpose flour, divided

½ cup heavy cream

1 egg, beaten

Vegetable oil for frying

Powdered sugar

MAKES 5 DOZEN BEIGNETS

1 Stir yeast into warm water in small bowl; set aside. Combine granulated sugar, shortening, salt and boiling water in bowl of stand mixer. Mix on low until shortening is melted and granulated sugar dissolves; cool to lukewarm. Add 3 cups flour, cream, egg and yeast mixture. Attach dough hook to mixer; mix on low 2 minutes. Add remaining flour ½ cup at a time, mixing on low 2 minutes or until dough clings to hook and cleans sides of bowl. Knead 2 minutes longer.

2 Transfer dough to lightly floured surface; roll into 24×10-inch rectangle. Cut dough into 2-inch squares with sharp knife.

3 Pour oil into large heavy saucepan or deep fryer to a depth of 2 inches. Heat oil to 360°F. Cook beignets in batches about 3 minutes, turning once; do not crowd pan. Drain on paper towels and sprinkle with powdered sugar.

NOTE: Doughnuts can be filled with custard, whipped cream or jelly using a pastry bag fitted with a small tip.

Orange **Cinnamon Rolls**

• • •

DOUGH

¼ cup warm water (105° to 110°F)

1 package (¼ ounce) active
dry yeast

½ cup milk

¼ cup granulated sugar

2 tablespoons butter, melted

1 egg

1 teaspoon vanilla

½ teaspoon salt

2½ to 2¾ cups all-purpose flour, divided

FILLING

⅓ cup granulated sugar

1 tablespoon grated orange peel

1 teaspoon ground cinnamon

2 tablespoons butter, melted

GLAZE

¾ cup powdered sugar

1 to 2 tablespoons orange juice

MAKES 24 SERVINGS

1 For dough, combine warm water and yeast in bowl of stand mixer; let stand 5 minutes.

2 Whisk milk, ¼ cup granulated sugar, 2 tablespoons butter, egg, vanilla and salt in medium bowl; add to yeast mixture. Add 2½ cups flour; stir on low until soft dough forms. Attach dough hook to mixer. Knead on low speed 5 to 8 minutes or until dough is smooth and elastic, adding enough remaining flour 1 tablespoon at a time if dough sticks to side of bowl.

3 Shape dough into a ball; place in large greased bowl. Turn to coat top. Cover and let rise in warm place (85°F) about 1 hour or until doubled. Spray two 8-inch round cake pans with nonstick cooking spray.

4 For filling, combine ⅓ cup granulated sugar, orange peel and cinnamon in small bowl. Divide dough into two pieces. Roll out each piece into 12×8-inch rectangle; brush each with 1 tablespoon melted butter. Sprinkle cinnamon-sugar mixture over dough. Roll up dough jelly-roll style from long side; cut each roll into 12 slices. Arrange slices, cut sides down, in prepared pans. Cover and let rise in warm place (85°F) about 1 hour or until doubled.

5 Preheat oven to 350°F. Bake, uncovered, 18 to 20 minutes or until rolls are golden brown. Cool in pans on wire racks 5 minutes. Remove to wire racks.

6 Meanwhile for glaze, whisk powdered sugar and 1 tablespoon orange juice in medium bowl until smooth. Add additional orange juice if needed until desired consistency is reached. Drizzle glaze over warm rolls; serve warm or at room temperature.

KitchenAid

Quick Breakfast **Empanadas**

• • •

½ pound bacon (about 10 slices)

1 package (about 15 ounces) refrigerated pie crusts

9 eggs, divided

1 teaspoon salt

Dash freshly ground black pepper

1 tablespoon butter

1¼ cups (5 ounces) Mexican blend shredded cheese, divided

4 tablespoons salsa

1 teaspoon water

MAKES 4 SERVINGS

1 Preheat oven to 425°F. Spray baking sheet with nonstick cooking spray. Cook bacon in large skillet over medium-high heat until crisp; drain on paper towels. Chop bacon into ¼-inch pieces. Unroll pie crusts; cut each crust in half and place on prepared baking sheet.

2 Beat 8 eggs, salt and pepper in medium bowl until well blended. Heat large skillet over medium heat. Add butter; tilt skillet to coat bottom. Sprinkle bacon evenly in skillet. Pour eggs into skillet and cook 2 minutes without stirring; gently stir until eggs form large curds and are still slightly moist. Transfer to plate to cool.

3 Spoon one fourth of egg mixture onto half of each crust. Sprinkle 1 cup cheese evenly over eggs. Top with salsa. Beat remaining egg and water in small bowl until well blended. Brush inside edges of crusts with egg mixture. Fold dough over egg mixture and seal edges with fork.

4 Brush tops of empanadas with remaining egg mixture and sprinkle with remaining ¼ cup cheese. Bake 15 to 20 minutes or until golden.

KitchenAid

French Toast with Orange Butter

• • •

⅓ cup whipped butter, softened

2 tablespoons orange marmalade

2 teaspoons honey

4 eggs, beaten

½ cup milk

2 tablespoons granulated sugar

1 teaspoon ground cinnamon

¼ teaspoon ground nutmeg

1 teaspoon vanilla

8 ounces French bread, cut diagonally into 8 slices

2 tablespoons vegetable oil, divided

1 tablespoon powdered sugar (optional)

MAKES 4 SERVINGS

1 For orange butter, blend butter, marmalade and honey in small bowl; set aside.

2 Whisk eggs, milk, granulated sugar, cinnamon, nutmeg and vanilla in medium bowl. Dip bread slices into egg mixture.

3 Heat 1 tablespoon oil in large skillet over medium heat, tilting to coat skillet. Add four bread slices; cook 3 minutes per side or until golden. Repeat with remaining 1 tablespoon oil and remaining four bread slices.

4 Top each slice with 1 tablespoon orange butter. Sprinkle with powdered sugar, if desired.

Upside-Down **Peach Corn Bread Cakes**

• • •

4 tablespoons butter, divided

½ cup packed brown sugar, divided

1 fresh peach, thinly sliced

2 packages (8½ ounces each) corn muffin and bread mix

½ cup milk

2 eggs

2 tablespoons vegetable oil

1¾ cups diced fresh peaches or thawed frozen diced peaches

MAKES 8 SERVINGS

1 Preheat oven to 400°F. Spray eight 8-ounce ramekins or muffin pan cups with nonstick cooking spray. Place 1½ teaspoons butter and 1 tablespoon brown sugar in each ramekin; top with fresh peach slices. Place ramekins on baking sheet.

2 Whisk corn muffin mix, milk, eggs and oil in large bowl. Stir in diced peaches. Pour ¾ cup batter into each ramekin.

3 Bake 20 minutes or until golden and toothpick inserted into centers comes out clean. Cool on wire rack 5 minutes. Run knife around edges of ramekins. Invert cakes onto serving plates.

KitchenAid

Cinnamon **French Toast Casserole**

● ● ●

1 large loaf French bread,
cut into 1½-inch slices

3½ cups milk

9 eggs

1½ cups granulated sugar, divided

1 tablespoon vanilla

½ teaspoon salt

6 to 8 medium baking apples,
such as McIntosh or Cortland, peeled
and sliced

1 teaspoon ground cinnamon

½ teaspoon ground nutmeg

Powdered sugar (optional)

MAKES 6 TO 8 SERVINGS

1 Spray 13×9-inch baking dish with nonstick cooking spray. Arrange bread slices in dish.

2 Whisk milk, eggs, 1 cup granulated sugar, vanilla and salt in large bowl until well blended. Pour half of mixture over bread. Layer apple slices over bread. Pour remaining half of egg mixture over apples.

3 Combine remaining ½ cup granulated sugar, cinnamon and nutmeg in small bowl; sprinkle over apples. Cover and refrigerate overnight.

4 Preheat oven to 350°F. Bake, uncovered, 1 hour or until eggs are set. Sprinkle with powdered sugar, if desired.

Ham and Egg **Breakfast Panini**

● ● ●

3 teaspoons vegetable oil, divided

¼ cup chopped green or red bell pepper

2 tablespoons sliced green onions

1 slice (1 ounce) smoked deli ham, chopped (about ¼ cup)

2 eggs

Salt and black pepper

4 slices multi-grain or whole grain bread

2 slices (¾ ounce each) Cheddar or Swiss cheese

MAKES 2 SERVINGS

1 Heat 1 teaspoon oil in small skillet over medium heat. Add bell pepper and green onions; cook and stir 4 minutes or until vegetables begin to soften. Add ham.

2 Combine eggs, salt and black pepper in small bowl; pour into skillet. Cook about 2 minutes, stirring occasionally until egg mixture is almost set.

3 Heat grill pan or medium skillet over medium heat. Top each of two bread slices with 1 cheese slice and half of egg mixture. Top with remaining bread slices. Brush outsides of sandwiches with remaining 2 teaspoons oil.

4 Grill sandwiches about 2 minutes per side or until toasted, pressing lightly with spatula. (If desired, cover pan with lid during last 2 minutes of cooking to melt cheese.) Cut sandwiches in half; serve immediately.

Mixed Berry **Whole-Grain Coffeecake**

• • •

1¼ cups all-purpose flour, divided

¾ cup old-fashioned oats

¾ cup packed brown sugar

3 tablespoons butter, softened

1 cup whole wheat flour

1 cup milk

¾ cup granulated sugar

¼ cup canola oil

1 egg, lightly beaten

1 tablespoon baking powder

1 teaspoon ground cinnamon

½ teaspoon salt

1½ cups frozen mixed berries, thawed and drained *or* 2 cups fresh berries

¼ cup chopped walnuts

MAKES 12 SERVINGS

1 Preheat oven to 350°F. Spray 9×5-inch loaf pan with nonstick cooking spray.

2 Combine ¼ cup all-purpose flour, oats, brown sugar and butter in small bowl. Mix with fork until crumbly; set aside.

3 Combine remaining 1 cup all-purpose flour, whole wheat flour, milk, granulated sugar, oil, egg, baking powder, cinnamon and salt in bowl of stand mixer. Beat at medium-low 1 to 2 minutes until well blended. Fold in berries. Spread batter in prepared pan. Sprinkle evenly with reserved oat mixture. Top with chopped walnuts.

4 Bake 38 to 40 minutes or until toothpick inserted into center comes out clean. Cool in pan on wire rack 10 minutes. Remove from pan to wire rack to cool. Serve warm.

Banana Walnut Muffins

• • •

1 cup coarsely chopped walnuts

2 cups all-purpose flour

2 teaspoons baking powder

½ teaspoon baking soda

¼ teaspoon salt

½ teaspoon ground cinnamon

¼ teaspoon nutmeg

3 ripe bananas

¼ cup sour cream

½ cup (1 stick) butter, softened

1 cup packed brown sugar

2 eggs, at room temperature

1 teaspoon vanilla

MAKES 12 MUFFINS

1 Preheat oven to 375°F. Line 12 standard (2½-inch) muffin pan cups with paper baking cups or spray with nonstick cooking spray.

2 Spread walnuts on baking sheet; bake 8 minutes, or until toasted, stirring occasionally. Remove from baking sheet; cool completely.

3 Sift flour, baking powder, baking soda, salt, cinnamon and nutmeg in medium bowl. Mash bananas in separate medium bowl; stir in sour cream until well blended.

4 Combine butter and brown sugar in bowl of stand mixer. Beat on medium-high until light and fluffy. Beat in eggs, one at a time, beating well after each addition. Beat in vanilla. Add banana mixture; beat until well blended. Add flour mixture; beat on low until combined. Stir in walnuts. Spoon batter evenly into prepared muffin cups.

5 Bake 25 to 30 minutes until toothpick inserted into centers comes out clean. Cool in pan on wire rack 5 minutes. Remove from pan to wire rack. Serve warm or cool completely. Store leftovers in airtight container at room temperature up to 4 days or freeze for longer storage.

KitchenAid

Gingerbread Coffeecake

● ● ●

2 tablespoons finely chopped walnuts

½ cup plus 2 tablespoons packed dark brown sugar, divided

⅔ cup whole wheat flour

¼ cup all-purpose flour

½ cup granulated sugar

3 teaspoons ground ginger

1½ teaspoons baking powder

1 teaspoon ground cinnamon

½ teaspoon salt

½ teaspoon ground cloves

¼ teaspoon baking soda

½ cup prune purée*

2 eggs

1 cup buttermilk

2 tablespoons canola oil

1 teaspoon vanilla

*Prune purée can be found in the baking aisle or baby food aisle at most supermarkets. It is a healthy alternative to baking with butter.

MAKES 8 SERVINGS

1 Preheat oven to 350°F. Spray 9-inch round cake pan with nonstick cooking spray. Combine walnuts and 2 tablespoons brown sugar in small bowl.

2 Combine remaining ½ cup brown sugar, whole wheat flour, all-purpose flour, granulated sugar, ginger, baking powder, cinnamon, salt, cloves and baking soda in large bowl. Combine prune purée and eggs in medium bowl. Whisk in buttermilk, oil and vanilla. Add to flour mixture; stir just until combined. Pour into prepared pan. Sprinkle with walnut mixture.

3 Bake 25 to 30 minutes or until toothpick inserted into center comes out clean. Cool in pan on wire rack 10 minutes. Remove to wire rack to cool.

Marmalade Muffins

• • •

2 cups all-purpose flour

2 teaspoons baking powder

¾ teaspoon salt

1 cup (2 sticks) butter, softened

1½ cups sugar

2 eggs

1½ teaspoons vanilla

1 cup orange marmalade,
plus additional for serving

1 cup buttermilk

MAKES 18 MUFFINS

1 Preheat oven to 350°F. Line 18 standard (2½-inch) muffin pan cups with paper baking cups.

2 Sift flour, baking powder and salt in medium bowl. Combine butter and sugar in bowl of stand mixer; beat on high about 5 minutes or until light and fluffy. Add eggs, one at a time, beating well after each addition. Add vanilla; mix well. Beat in half of flour mixture on low just until moistened. Beat in 1 cup marmalade and remaining flour mixture. Stir in buttermilk on low; do not overmix. Spoon batter evenly into prepared muffin cups.

3 Bake 20 to 25 minutes or until edges are golden brown and toothpick inserted into centers comes out clean. Top with additional marmalade.

Cherry-Lemon **Poppy Seed Muffins**

● ● ●

2 cups all-purpose flour

1 cup sugar

1 tablespoon baking powder

1 teaspoon salt

¾ cup buttermilk

¼ cup vegetable oil

¼ cup (½ stick) butter, melted

2 eggs, lightly beaten

1 tablespoon grated lemon peel

1 tablespoon lemon juice

1 teaspoon vanilla

½ cup dried cherries, chopped

½ cup chopped pecans

2 tablespoons poppy seeds

MAKES 12 MUFFINS

1 Preheat oven to 350°F. Spray 12 standard (2½-inch) muffin pan cups with nonstick cooking spray.

2 Combine flour, sugar, baking powder and salt in large bowl. Make well in center. Combine buttermilk, oil, butter, eggs, lemon peel, lemon juice and vanilla in medium bowl. Pour into flour mixture; stir just until blended. Stir in cherries, pecans and poppy seeds just until blended. Spoon batter evenly into prepared muffin cups.

3 Bake 20 to 24 minutes or until golden brown and toothpick inserted into centers comes out clean. Cool in pan on wire rack 5 minutes. Remove to wire rack to cool completely. Store in airtight container.

Chocolate Chunk Coffeecake

• • •

1¾ cups all-purpose flour

1 teaspoon baking powder

1 teaspoon baking soda

½ teaspoon salt

¾ cup packed brown sugar

½ cup (1 stick) butter, softened

3 eggs

1 teaspoon vanilla

1 cup sour cream

1 package (about 11 ounces) semisweet chocolate chunks

1 cup chopped nuts

MAKES ABOUT 18 SERVINGS

1 Preheat oven to 350°F. Spray 13×9-inch baking pan with nonstick cooking spray.

2 Combine flour, baking powder, baking soda and salt in medium bowl. Combine brown sugar and butter in bowl of stand mixer; beat on medium-high until light and fluffy. Add eggs, one at a time, beating well after each addition. Beat in vanilla until well blended. Alternately add flour mixture and sour cream; beat on low until blended. Stir in chocolate chunks and nuts. Spread batter evenly in prepared pan.

3 Bake 25 to 35 minutes or until toothpick inserted into center comes out clean. Cool completely in pan on wire rack.

Carrot and Oat Muffins

● ● ●

1 cup minus 2 tablespoons
old-fashioned oats

¾ cup all-purpose flour

¾ cup whole wheat flour

⅓ cup sugar

1½ teaspoons baking powder

1 teaspoon ground cinnamon

½ teaspoon baking soda

¼ teaspoon salt

½ cup milk

½ cup unsweetened applesauce

2 eggs, beaten

1 tablespoon canola oil

½ cup shredded carrot (1 large carrot)

¼ cup finely chopped walnuts (optional)

MAKES 12 MUFFINS

1 Preheat oven to 350°F. Spray 12 standard (2½-inch) muffin pan cups with nonstick cooking spray.

2 Combine oats, all-purpose flour, whole wheat flour, sugar, baking powder, cinnamon, baking soda and salt in medium bowl. Whisk milk, applesauce, eggs and oil in large bowl. Stir in carrot. Add flour mixture; stir just until moistened. Do not beat. Spoon batter evenly into prepared muffin cups. Sprinkle 1 teaspoon walnuts over each muffin, if desired.

3 Bake 20 to 22 minutes or until muffins are golden brown and toothpick inserted into centers comes out clean. Cool in muffin pan 5 minutes. Remove from pan to wire rack to cool completely.

NOTE: These muffins are best eaten the same day they are made.

KitchenAid

Blueberry Macadamia Nut
Swirl Coffeecake

• • •

1¾ cups all-purpose flour

½ cup whole wheat flour

¾ cup packed brown sugar

¾ cup (1½ sticks) cold butter, cut into small pieces

1 teaspoon baking powder

½ teaspoon baking soda

¼ teaspoon salt

¾ cup buttermilk

1 egg

1 cup blueberry pie filling

¾ cup chopped macadamia nuts

MAKES ABOUT 18 SERVINGS

1 Preheat oven to 350°F. Spray 13×9-inch baking pan with nonstick cooking spray.

2 Combine all-purpose flour, whole wheat flour, brown sugar and butter in bowl of stand mixer; mix on low 3 minutes or until mixture forms pea-size pieces. Stop and scrape bowl. Remove ½ cup flour mixture.

3 Add baking powder, baking soda and salt to flour mixture in bowl. Mix on low 30 seconds. Add buttermilk and egg; mix on low 30 seconds or just until moistened. Do not overbeat. Spoon batter into prepared pan. Drop blueberry filling by tablespoonfuls on top of batter; swirl into batter. Sprinkle with nuts and reserved flour mixture.

4 Bake 30 to 40 minutes or until topping is golden brown and filling is bubbly. Cool completely in pan on wire rack.

Whole Wheat **Pumpkin Muffins**

• • •

1½ cups whole wheat flour

¼ cup sugar

1 teaspoon salt

1 teaspoon ground allspice

1 teaspoon ground nutmeg

¾ teaspoon baking powder

½ teaspoon baking soda

¾ cup canned solid-pack pumpkin

½ cup canola oil

½ cup honey

½ cup thawed frozen apple juice concentrate

½ cup chopped walnuts

½ cup golden raisins

MAKES 12 MUFFINS

1 Preheat oven to 350°F. Spray 12 standard (2½-inch) muffin pan cups with nonstick cooking spray.

2 Combine flour, sugar, salt, allspice, nutmeg, baking powder and baking soda in medium bowl; mix well. Combine pumpkin, oil, honey and apple juice concentrate in large bowl. Add flour mixture; stir just until moistened. Stir in walnuts and raisins. Spoon batter evenly into prepared muffin cups.

3 Bake 12 to 15 minutes or until toothpick inserted into centers comes out clean. Remove to wire rack to cool completely.

KitchenAid

Raspberry Corn Muffins

● ● ●

1 cup all-purpose flour

¾ cup cornmeal

2 teaspoons baking powder

½ teaspoon baking soda

¼ teaspoon salt

1 egg, beaten

1 cup sour cream

⅓ cup thawed frozen unsweetened apple juice concentrate

1½ cups fresh or frozen raspberries

⅔ cup whipped cream cheese

2 tablespoons raspberry fruit spread

MAKES 12 MUFFINS

1 Preheat oven to 350°F. Spray 12 standard (2½-inch) muffin pan cups with nonstick cooking spray.

2 Combine flour, cornmeal, baking powder, baking soda and salt in small bowl. Whisk egg, sour cream and apple juice concentrate in medium bowl. Add flour mixture; stir just until dry ingredients are moistened. Do not overmix. Gently stir in raspberries. Spoon batter evenly into prepared muffin cups.

3 Bake 18 to 20 minutes or until tops are brown and toothpick inserted into centers comes out clean. Cool in pan on wire rack 5 minutes. Remove from pan to wire rack to cool slightly.

4 Combine cream cheese and fruit spread in small serving bowl. Serve with warm muffins.

Blueberry Poppy Seed Coffeecake

• • •

1½ cups all-purpose flour

½ cup sugar

1 teaspoon baking powder

½ teaspoon baking soda

¼ teaspoon salt

¼ cup (½ stick) cold butter, cut into small pieces

1 tablespoon poppy seeds

¾ cup buttermilk

1 egg

1 teaspoon vanilla

1 teaspoon grated lemon peel

1 cup fresh blueberries

MAKES 8 SERVINGS

1 Preheat oven to 350°F. Spray 9-inch round cake pan with nonstick cooking spray.

2 Combine flour, sugar, baking powder, baking soda and salt in bowl of stand mixer. Add butter; mix on low until mixture resembles coarse crumbs. Stir in poppy seeds.

3 Whisk buttermilk, egg, vanilla and lemon peel in small bowl until blended. Stir buttermilk mixture into flour mixture on low just until moistened. Spread half of batter into prepared pan; top with blueberries. Drop remaining batter in eight dollops onto blueberries.

4 Bake 30 to 35 minutes or until top is golden brown. Cool in pan on wire rack 15 minutes. Serve warm.

KitchenAid

Cranberry Chocolate Chunk Muffins

• • •

2 cups all-purpose flour

¾ cup coarsely chopped pecans

½ cup granulated sugar

½ cup coarsely chopped dried cranberries

1 semisweet chocolate bar (4 ounces), chopped into ½-inch chunks

2 teaspoons baking powder

½ teaspoon salt

½ cup orange juice

½ cup vegetable oil

2 eggs, lightly beaten

¾ teaspoon orange extract

MAKES 12 MUFFINS

1 Preheat oven to 375°F. Spray 12 standard (2½-inch) muffin pan cups with nonstick cooking spray or line with paper baking cups.

2 Combine flour, pecans, sugar, cranberries, chocolate, baking powder and salt in large bowl; make well in center. Combine juice, oil, eggs and orange extract in small bowl; mix well. Add to dry ingredients; stir just until moistened. Divide batter evenly among prepared muffin cups.

3 Bake 18 to 22 minutes or until toothpick inserted into centers comes out clean. Cool in pan on wire rack 5 minutes. Remove to wire rack. Serve warm. Store in airtight container.

breads, biscuits and scones

Coconut Scones with Orange Butter

· · · ·

1¾ cups all-purpose flour

½ teaspoon salt

1 tablespoon baking powder

2 tablespoons sugar

5 tablespoons cold butter, cut into small pieces

1 cup heavy cream, divided

½ cup plus ⅓ cup sweetened shredded coconut, divided

1 egg

2 tablespoons milk

2 teaspoons grated orange peel

Orange Butter (recipe follows)

MAKES 8 SCONES

1 Preheat oven to 400°F. Line baking sheet with parchment paper.

2 Combine flour, salt, baking powder and sugar in bowl of stand mixer. Add butter; mix on low until mixture resembles coarse crumbs. Whisk ¾ cup cream, ½ cup coconut, egg, milk and orange peel in small bowl. Add to flour mixture; mix on low just until dough forms.

3 Transfer dough to lightly floured surface and pat into 8-inch circle about ¾-inch thick. Cut into eight triangles; place 2 inches apart on prepared baking sheet. Brush tops of scones with remaining ¼ cup cream; sprinkle with remaining ⅓ cup coconut.

4 Bake 12 to 15 minutes or until scones are golden brown and coconut is toasted. Remove to wire rack; cool 15 minutes. Prepare Orange Butter; serve with warm scones.

Orange Butter

MAKES ABOUT 1 CUP

½ cup (1 stick) butter, softened

2 tablespoons freshly squeezed orange juice

1 tablespoon grated orange peel

2 teaspoons sugar

Combine all ingredients in bowl of stand mixer. Beat on medium until creamy and well blended.

KitchenAid

Mustard Beer Biscuits

• • •

2 cups all-purpose flour

2 teaspoons baking powder

³/₄ teaspoon salt

¼ cup cold shortening

¼ cup (½ stick) cold butter, cut into small pieces

½ cup beer

1 tablespoon plus 1 teaspoon mustard, divided

1 tablespoon milk

MAKES 12 BISCUITS

1 Preheat oven to 425°F. Spray baking sheet with nonstick cooking spray or line with parchment paper.

2 Combine flour, baking powder and salt in bowl of stand mixer. Add shortening and butter; mix on low until mixture resembles coarse crumbs. Combine beer and 1 tablespoon mustard in small bowl; stir into flour mixture on low just until blended. Knead dough 8 to 10 times on floured surface. Pat dough to ½-inch thickness. Cut dough with 2-inch round biscuit cutter; gather scraps and cut additional biscuits. Place 1 inch apart on prepared baking sheet. Combine remaining 1 teaspoon mustard and milk in small bowl and brush over tops.

3 Bake 13 to 15 minutes or until lightly browned. Remove to wire rack. Serve warm..

Cranberry and White Chocolate Scones

• • •

1 cup all-purpose flour

1 cup whole wheat flour

¼ cup plus 1 tablespoon sugar, divided

2 teaspoons baking powder

½ teaspoon salt

½ teaspoon ground nutmeg

6 tablespoons cold butter, cut into small pieces

1 cup dried cranberries

1 cup white chocolate chips

2 eggs

⅓ cup plus 1 tablespoon heavy cream, divided

Grated peel of 1 orange

MAKES 8 SCONES

1 Preheat oven to 425°F. Line baking sheet with parchment paper.

2 Combine all-purpose flour, whole wheat flour, ¼ cup sugar, baking powder, salt and nutmeg in bowl of stand mixer. Add butter; mix on low until mixture resembles coarse crumbs. Stir in cranberries and white chips. Beat eggs in small bowl; whisk in ⅓ cup cream and orange peel. Add to flour mixture; mix on low just until dough forms.

3 Knead dough 8 to 10 times on lightly floured surface. Shape dough into disk; place on prepared baking sheet and press into 9-inch circle. Score dough into eight wedges with sharp knife. Brush with remaining 1 tablespoon cream; sprinkle with remaining 1 tablespoon sugar.

4 Bake 20 to 23 minutes or until edges are lightly browned and toothpick inserted into centers comes out clean. Cut into wedges along score lines. Remove to wire rack to cool completely.

Simply Scones

• • •

2 cups all-purpose flour

2 tablespoons sugar

2 teaspoons baking powder

½ teaspoon salt

⅓ cup butter, softened

2 eggs, divided

½ cup heavy cream

1 teaspoon water

MAKES 16 SCONES

1 Preheat oven to 425°F. Grease baking sheets or line with parchment paper.

2 Combine flour, sugar, baking powder, salt and butter in bowl of stand mixer; mix on medium-low 30 seconds or until blended. Add 1 egg and cream; mix 30 seconds or until soft dough forms.

3 Knead dough three times on lightly floured surface. Divide dough in half. Pat each half into circle about ½-inch thick. Cut each circle into eight wedges; place 2 inches apart on prepared baking sheets. Whisk remaining egg and water in small bowl; brush over scones.

4 Bake 10 to 12 minutes or until golden brown. Serve immediately.

English-Style Scones

• • •

2 cups all-purpose flour

2 teaspoons baking powder

¼ teaspoon salt

¼ cup (½ stick) cold butter, cut into small pieces

¼ cup finely chopped pitted dates

¼ cup golden raisins or currants

3 eggs, divided

½ cup heavy cream

1½ teaspoons vanilla

1 teaspoon water

Orange marmalade

Crème fraîche or softly whipped cream

MAKES 6 SCONES

1 Preheat oven to 375°F. Lightly grease large baking sheet or line with parchment paper.

2 Combine flour, baking powder and salt in bowl of stand mixer. Add butter; mix on low until mixture resembles coarse crumbs. Stir in dates and raisins. Whisk 2 eggs, cream and vanilla in small bowl. Add to flour mixture; mix on low just until moistened.

3 Knead dough four times on lightly floured surface. Place dough on prepared cookie sheet; pat into 8-inch circle. Score dough into six wedges with sharp knife, cutting three fourths through dough. Beat remaining egg and water in small bowl; brush over scones.

4 Bake 18 to 20 minutes or until golden brown. Cool on wire rack 5 minutes. Cut into wedges along score lines. Serve warm with marmalade and crème fraîche.

Glazed Espresso **Chocolate Marble Bread**

● ● ●

4 cups all-purpose flour

2 teaspoons baking powder

1 teaspoon baking soda

½ teaspoon salt

1½ cups (3 sticks) butter, softened

2 cups sugar

4 eggs

1 tablespoon vanilla

2 cups sour cream

1 tablespoon plus ½ teaspoon instant espresso powder or instant coffee granules, divided

5 tablespoons hot water, divided

¼ cup unsweetened cocoa powder

½ cup semisweet chocolate chips

¼ cup heavy cream

MAKES 3 LOAVES

1 Preheat oven to 350°F. Spray three 8×4-inch loaf pans with nonstick cooking spray.

2 Combine flour, baking powder, baking soda and salt in small bowl. Combine butter and sugar in bowl of stand mixer; beat on medium-high 5 minutes or until light and fluffy. Beat in eggs, one at a time, and vanilla. Beat in half of flour mixture on low until well blended. Add sour cream; beat about 1 minute or until well blended. Beat in remaining flour mixture.

3 Remove half of batter to medium bowl. Stir 1 tablespoon espresso powder into 2 tablespoons hot water until smooth; add to half of batter and mix well. Blend cocoa and remaining 3 tablespoons water in small bowl until smooth; stir into remaining half of batter until well blended. Drop large spoonfuls of each batter alternately into prepared loaf pans. Swirl batter once or twice with tip of knife.

4 Bake 45 to 50 minutes or until toothpick inserted into centers comes out clean. Cool in pans on wire racks 10 minutes. Remove from pans; cool completely on wire racks.

5 Combine chocolate chips, cream and remaining ½ teaspoon espresso powder in medium microwavable bowl. Microwave on HIGH 20 seconds; stir until smooth. Microwave at additional 15-second intervals until chocolate is melted and mixture is smooth. Drizzle glaze over loaves.

Pepperoni Cheese Bread

• • •

1 cup warm beer

½ cup warm milk

1 package (¼ ounce) active dry yeast

2¼ cups all-purpose flour, divided

1 cup rye flour

1 tablespoon dried basil

1 teaspoon sugar

1 teaspoon salt

1 teaspoon red pepper flakes

1 cup (4 ounces) shredded sharp Cheddar cheese

1 cup finely chopped pepperoni

1 tablespoon olive oil

MAKES 2 LOAVES

1 Heat beer and milk in small saucepan over medium-low heat to 105° to 110°F. Transfer to bowl of stand mixer; stir in yeast. Add 2 cups all-purpose flour, rye flour, basil, sugar, salt and red pepper flakes; mix on low until smooth Replace flat beater with dough hook. Add cheese and pepperoni. Knead on low 5 to 6 minutes or until smooth and elastic, adding additional all-purpose flour by tablespoons if dough sticks to side of bowl. Shape dough into ball. Place in large greased bowl; turn to grease top. Cover and let rise in warm place 1 hour or until doubled.

2 Grease baking sheets. Punch down dough; divide in half. Shape into two 12-inch-long loaves. Place on prepared baking sheets. Cover and let rise in warm place 45 minutes or until doubled.

3 Preheat oven to 350°F. Bake 30 to 35 minutes or until golden brown. Brush with oil. Cool on wire rack 20 minutes. Serve warm or cool completely.

○ **TIP**

SERVE BREAD WITH AN OREGANO-INFUSED DIPPING OIL. COMBINE 2 TABLESPOONS OLIVE OIL, ½ TEASPOON BLACK PEPPER, 1 TABLESPOON CHOPPED GREEN OLIVES AND 1 SPRIG FRESH OREGANO. LET SIT SEVERAL HOURS BEFORE SERVING TO BLEND FLAVORS.

Whole Grain
Wheat Bread

• • •

2 cups warm water
(105° to 115°F)

2 packages (¼ ounce each) active
dry yeast

⅓ cup plus 1 tablespoon packed brown
sugar, divided

5 to 6 cups whole wheat flour, divided

¾ cup powdered milk

2 teaspoons salt

⅓ cup vegetable oil

MAKES 2 LOAVES

1 Combine water, yeast and 1 tablespoon brown sugar in small bowl.

2 Place 4 cups flour, powdered milk, remaining ⅓ cup brown sugar and salt in bowl of stand mixer; attach dough hook. Mix on low 15 seconds. Gradually add yeast mixture and oil to flour mixture, mixing about 1½ minutes. Add remaining flour, ½ cup at a time, mixing on low about 2 minutes or until dough clings to hook* and cleans sides of bowl. Knead on low 2 minutes longer. Shape dough into ball. Place in large greased bowl; turn to grease top. Cover and let rise in warm place 1 hour or until doubled.

3 Grease two 8×4-inch loaf pans. Punch down dough; divide in half. Shape each half into loaf. Place in prepared pans. Cover and let rise in warm place 1 hour or until doubled.

4 Preheat oven to 400°F. Bake 15 minutes. *Reduce oven temperature to 350°F. Bake 30 minutes.* Immediately remove from pans; cool completely on wire racks.

Dough may not form a ball on hook. However, as long as hook comes in contact with dough, kneading will be accomplished. Do not add more than the maximum amount of flour specified or a dry loaf will result.

Garlic **Pull-Apart Bread**

● ● ●

1½ cups water

½ cup milk

½ cup (1 stick) butter, divided

6 to 7 cups all-purpose
flour, divided

3 tablespoons sugar

2 tablespoons garlic salt, divided

2 packages (¼ ounce each) active dry
yeast

MAKES 2 LOAVES

1 Heat water, milk and ¼ cup butter in small saucepan over medium-low heat to 120° to 130°F (butter may not melt completely).

2 Combine 5 cups flour, sugar, 1 tablespoon garlic salt and yeast in bowl of stand mixer; attach dough hook. Mix on low 15 seconds. Gradually add milk mixture, mixing about 1½ minutes. Add remaining flour, ½ cup at a time, mixing on low until dough clings to hook and cleans sides of bowl. Knead on low 2 minutes longer. Shape dough into ball. Place in large greased bowl; turn to grease top. Cover and let rise in warm place 1 hour or until doubled.

3 Grease two 8×4-inch loaf pans. Melt remaining ¼ cup butter in small saucepan over low heat; stir in remaining 1 tablespoon garlic salt. Punch down dough; divide in half. Roll each half into 12×8×¼-inch rectangle. Brush butter mixture over dough. Cut each rectangle into four 8×3-inch strips. Stack strips and cut into four 3×2-inch strips. Stand dough strips in prepared pans. Cover and let rise in warm place 1 hour or until doubled.

4 Preheat oven to 400°F. Bake 30 to 35 minutes or until tops are golden brown. Immediately remove from pans; cool on wire racks.

Soft **Beer Pretzels**

● ● ●

⅔ cup beer

6½ cups water, divided

2 tablespoons vegetable oil

3¼ cups all-purpose flour, divided

1 package (¼ ounce) active dry yeast

1 teaspoon salt

2 tablespoons baking soda

1 egg, beaten

Kosher salt

○ **TIP**

WHEN SHAPING PRETZELS, MAKE LARGE EXAGGERATED LOOPS. SMALLER LOOPS WILL CLOSE WHEN BOILED.

MAKES 12 PRETZELS

1 Heat beer, ½ cup water and oil in small saucepan to 120°F. Combine 3 cups flour, yeast and salt in bowl of stand mixer. Add beer mixture; mix on low until moistened. Stir in remaining flour, 1 tablespoon at a time, until soft dough forms. Replace flat beater with dough hook; knead on low 5 to 6 minutes or until smooth and elastic. Shape dough into ball. Place in large greased bowl; turn to grease top. Cover and let rise in warm place 15 minutes.

2 Grease two baking sheets. Divide dough in half; cut each half into six pieces. With lightly floured hands, roll each piece into 14-inch rope. (Cover remaining dough while working to prevent it from drying out.) Twist each rope into pretzel shape, pressing edges to seal. Place on prepared baking sheets. Cover and let rise in warm place 15 minutes.

3 Preheat oven to 400°F. Bring 6 cups water to a boil in large saucepan; stir in baking soda. Working in batches, gently lower pretzels into boiling water; cook 30 seconds, turning once. Remove pretzels with slotted spoon to wire racks coated with nonstick cooking spray. Brush with egg and sprinkle with salt. Bake on ungreased baking sheets 10 minutes or until golden brown. Cool on wire racks.

Chili **Corn Bread**

• • •

1 teaspoon vegetable oil

¼ cup chopped red bell pepper

¼ cup chopped green bell pepper

2 small jalapeño peppers, seeded and minced

2 cloves garlic, minced

¾ cup corn

1½ cups yellow cornmeal

½ cup all-purpose flour

2 tablespoons sugar

2 teaspoons baking powder

½ teaspoon baking soda

½ teaspoon ground cumin

½ teaspoon salt

1½ cups buttermilk

1 egg

2 egg whites

¼ cup (½ stick) butter, melted

MAKES 12 SERVINGS

1 Preheat oven to 425°F. Spray 8-inch square baking pan with nonstick cooking spray.

2 Heat oil in small skillet over medium heat. Add bell peppers, jalapeños and garlic; cook and stir 3 to 4 minutes or until peppers are tender. Stir in corn; cook 1 to 2 minutes. Remove from heat.

3 Combine cornmeal, flour, sugar, baking powder, baking soda, cumin and salt in large bowl. Add buttermilk, egg, egg whites and butter; mix until blended. Stir in corn mixture. Pour batter into prepared pan.

4 Bake 25 to 30 minutes or until golden brown and toothpick inserted into center comes out clean. Cool in pan on wire rack. Serve warm or cool completely.

Crunchy **Whole Grain** Bread

• • •

1½ cups water

⅓ cup honey

1 tablespoon salt

2 tablespoons vegetable oil

½ cup warm water (105° to 115°F)

2 packages (¼ ounce each) active dry yeast

2 to 2½ cups whole wheat flour, divided

1 cup bread flour

1 cup old-fashioned oats, plus additional for garnish

½ cup hulled pumpkin or sunflower seeds

½ cup assorted grains and seeds

1 egg white

1 tablespoon water

MAKES 2 LOAVES

1 Heat 1½ cups water, honey, salt and oil in medium saucepan to 115° to 120°F. Combine warm water and yeast in bowl of stand mixer; let stand 5 minutes. Stir in honey mixture, 1 cup whole wheat flour and bread flour on low 2 minutes or until combined. Gradually stir in 1 cup oats, pumpkin seeds, grains and remaining 1 cup whole wheat flour, ½ cup at a time, until dough begins to form a ball. Replace flat beater with dough hook. Knead on low 7 to 10 minutes or until dough is smooth and elastic.

2 Shape dough into ball. Place in greased bowl; turn to grease top. Cover and let rise in warm place 1½ to 2 hours or until doubled.

3 Grease two 9×5-inch loaf pans. Punch down dough; divide in half. Shape each half into loaf; place in prepared pans. Cover and let rise in warm place 1 hour or until almost doubled.

4 Preheat oven to 375°F. Whisk egg white and 1 tablespoon water in small bowl; brush over loaves. Sprinkle with additional oats. Bake 35 to 45 minutes or until loaves sound hollow when tapped. Immediately remove from pans to wire rack to cool completely.

○ **TIP**

TRY ADDING COOKED QUINOA, BROWN RICE, MILLET OR WHEAT BERRIES.

Three-Grain Bread

• • •

1 cup milk

2 tablespoons honey

3 teaspoons olive oil

1 teaspoon salt

1 cup whole wheat flour

¾ cup all-purpose flour

1 package (¼ ounce) active
dry yeast

½ cup old-fashioned oats, plus additional
for garnish

¼ cup whole grain cornmeal, plus
additional for pan

1 egg

1 tablespoon water

MAKES 1 LOAF

1 Heat milk, honey, olive oil and salt in small saucepan over low heat to 110°
to 120°F. Combine whole wheat flour, all-purpose flour and yeast in bowl
of stand mixer. Stir in milk mixture; beat on high 3 minutes. Mix in ½ cup
oats and ¼ cup cornmeal on low. If dough is too wet, add additional flour
by teaspoonfuls until it begins to come together. Replace flat beater with
dough hook. Knead on medium 5 minutes or until dough is smooth and
elastic. Shape dough into ball. Place in large greased bowl; turn to grease
top. Cover and let rise in warm place about 1 hour or until dough is puffy
and does not spring back when touched.

2 Lightly dust baking sheet with additional cornmeal. Punch down dough;
shape into 8-inch-long loaf. Cover and let rise in warm place 45 minutes or
until almost doubled.

3 Preheat oven to 375°F. Make shallow slash down center of loaf with sharp
knife. Whisk egg and water in small bowl; brush over loaf and sprinkle with
additional oats. Bake 30 minutes or until loaf sounds hollow when tapped
(internal temperature of 200°F). Remove to wire rack to cool.

Basic **White Bread**

• • •

½ cup milk

3 tablespoons sugar

3 tablespoons butter

2 teaspoons salt

1½ cups warm water
(105° to 115°F)

2 packages (¼ ounce each)
active dry yeast

5 to 6 cups all-purpose flour, divided

MAKES 2 LOAVES

1 Heat milk, sugar, butter and salt in small saucepan over low heat until butter melts and sugar dissolves. Cool to lukewarm.

2 Combine warm water and yeast in bowl of stand mixer; attach dough hook. Add milk mixture and 4½ cups flour; mix on low about 1 minute. Add remaining flour, ½ cup at a time, mixing about 2 minutes or until dough clings to hook and cleans sides of bowl. Knead on low about 2 minutes longer or until dough is smooth, elastic and slightly sticky. Shape dough into ball. Place in greased bowl; turn to grease top. Cover and let rise in warm place about 1 hour or until doubled.

3 Grease two 8×4-inch loaf pans. Punch down dough; divide in half. Roll out each half into 12×8-inch rectangle. Roll up from short side; place in prepared pans. Cover and let rise in warm place about 1 hour or until doubled.

4 Preheat oven to 400°F. Bake about 30 minutes or until golden brown. Immediately remove from pans to wire racks to cool.

CINNAMON BREAD: Prepare Basic White Bread through rolling out dough in step 3. Combine ½ cup sugar and 2 teaspoons cinnamon in small bowl. Spread 1 tablespoon softened butter over each piece of dough; sprinkle with cinnamon-sugar. Roll up from short side; place in prepared pans. Cover and let rise in warm place about 1 hour or until doubled. Brush tops with beaten egg white. Bake at 375°F 40 to 45 minutes or until golden brown. Immediately remove from pans to wire racks to cool.

SIXTY-MINUTE ROLLS: Prepare Basic White Bread through step 2, increasing yeast to 3 packages and sugar to ¼ cup. Divide dough into 24 pieces and shape into balls, or shape into curlicues or cloverleafs (see below); place 2 inches apart on greased baking sheet. Cover and let rise in slightly warm oven (90°F) about 15 minutes. Remove rolls and preheat oven to 425°F. Bake 12 minutes or until golden brown. Cool on wire racks.

CURLICUES: Divide dough in half; roll out each half into 12×9-inch rectangle. Cut 12 (1-inch-wide) strips. Roll each strip tightly to form a coil, tucking ends underneath.

CLOVERLEAFS: Divide dough into 24 pieces; shape into balls and place in greased muffin pan cups. Cut in half and then into quarters with scissors.

Boston Black **Coffee Bread**

• • •

½ cup rye flour

½ cup cornmeal

½ cup whole wheat flour

1 teaspoon baking soda

½ teaspoon salt

¾ cup strong brewed coffee,
room temperature or cold

⅓ cup molasses

¼ cup canola oil

¾ cup raisins

MAKES 1 LOAF

1 Preheat oven to 325°F. Butter and flour 9×5-inch loaf pan.

2 Combine rye flour, cornmeal, whole wheat flour, baking soda and salt in large bowl. Stir in coffee, molasses and oil until mixture forms thick batter. Fold in raisins. Pour batter into prepared pan.

3 Bake 50 minutes or until toothpick inserted into center comes out clean. Cool completely in pan on wire rack.

○ **TIP**

TO COOL HOT COFFEE, POUR OVER 2 ICE CUBES IN A MEASURING CUP TO MEASURE ¾ CUP TOTAL. LET STAND 10 MINUTES TO COOL.

KitchenAid

Crusty **Pizza Dough**

• • •

1 cup warm water (105° to 115°F)

1 package (¼ ounce) active dry yeast

2½ to 3½ cups all-purpose flour, divided

2 teaspoons olive oil, plus additional for pan

½ teaspoon salt

1 tablespoon cornmeal

Toppings: tomato slices, shredded fresh basil, fresh mozzarella and red pepper flakes

MAKES 1 PIZZA CRUST

1 Combine warm water and yeast in bowl of stand mixer; attach dough hook. Add 2½ cups flour, 2 teaspoons olive oil and salt; mix on low 1 minute. Add remaining flour, ½ cup at a time, mixing about 2 minutes or until dough clings to hook and cleans sides of bowl. Knead on low 2 minutes longer.

2 Shape dough into ball. Place in greased bowl; turn to grease top. Cover and let rise in warm place about 1 hour or until doubled.

3 Preheat oven to 450°F. Brush 14-inch pizza pan with additional oil; sprinkle with cornmeal. Punch down dough. Press dough into pan. Top with desired toppings. Bake 15 to 20 minutes.

New York **Rye Bread**

• • •

2 cups warm water (105° to 115°F)

⅓ cup packed brown sugar

2 tablespoons vegetable oil

1 tablespoon salt

1 package (¼ ounce) active dry yeast

2 to 2½ cups bread flour, divided

1 tablespoon caraway seeds

2 cups rye flour

1 cup whole wheat flour

Shortening

Cornmeal

MAKES 2 LOAVES

1 Combine warm water, brown sugar, oil, salt and yeast in bowl of stand mixer. Add 2 cups bread flour and caraway seeds; mix on low about 2 minutes. Gradually stir in rye flour and whole wheat flour, ½ cup at a time, and enough remaining bread flour until dough begins to form a ball. Replace flat beater with dough hook. Knead on low 7 to 10 minutes or until dough is smooth and elastic.

2 Shape dough into ball. Place in greased bowl; turn to grease top. Cover and let rise in warm place 1½ to 2 hours or until doubled.

3 Grease large baking sheet with shortening. Sprinkle with cornmeal. Punch down dough; divide in half. Shape each half into 10-inch-long oblong loaf. Place on prepared baking sheet. Cover and let rise in warm place 45 to 60 minutes or until almost doubled.

4 Preheat oven to 375°F. Spray or brush loaves with cool water; sprinkle lightly with bread flour. Carefully cut three ¼-inch-deep slashes on top of loaf with serrated knife.

5 Bake 25 to 30 minutes or until loaves sound hollow when tapped. Remove to wire rack to cool.

○ **TIP**

NEW YORK RYE BREAD IS A LIGHT RYE BREAD, TYPICALLY SHAPED INTO OBLONG OR ROUND LOAVES. TRY IT FOR DELICIOUS DELI MEAT SANDWICHES OR GRILLED CHEESE.

Classic Deli **Pumpernickel Bread**

• • •

1 cup strong coffee,* cold or at room
temperature

½ cup finely chopped onion

½ cup molasses

2 tablespoons butter

1 tablespoon salt

½ cup warm water (105° to 115°F)

2 packages (¼ ounce each)
active dry yeast

2½ cups bread flour, divided

1 cup whole wheat flour

¼ cup unsweetened cocoa powder

1 tablespoon caraway seeds

2 cups medium rye flour

Cornmeal

*Use fresh brewed coffee or instant coffee
granules prepared according to package
directions.

MAKES 2 LOAVES

1 Heat coffee, onion, molasses, butter and salt in medium saucepan
to 115° to 120°F.

2 Combine warm water and yeast in bowl of stand mixer; let stand
5 minutes. Stir in coffee mixture, 2 cups bread flour, whole wheat flour,
cocoa and caraway seeds on low about 2 minutes or until combined.
Gradually stir in rye flour, ½ cup at a time, and enough remaining bread
flour until dough begins to form ball. Replace flat beater with dough hook.
Knead on low 7 to 10 minutes or until dough is smooth and elastic.

3 Shape dough into ball. Place in greased bowl; turn to grease top. Cover
and let rise in warm place 2 hours or until doubled.

4 Grease large baking sheet; sprinkle with cornmeal. Punch down dough;
divide in half. Shape each half into round, slightly flattened loaf. Place on
prepared baking sheet. Cover and let rise in warm place 1 hour or until
almost doubled.

5 Preheat oven to 375°F. Bake 30 to 35 minutes or until loaves sound
hollow when tapped. Remove to wire rack to cool.

KitchenAid

Egg **Bagels**

• • •

½ to ¾ cup warm water
(105° to 115°F), divided

1 package (¼ ounce)
active dry yeast

2 tablespoons plus
1 teaspoon sugar, divided

2½ cups all-purpose flour

1 tablespoon canola oil

1 teaspoon salt

2 eggs, divided

2 quarts water

2 tablespoons cold water

MAKES 1 DOZEN BAGELS

1 Combine ¼ cup warm water, yeast and 1 teaspoon sugar in small bowl; let stand 5 minutes.

2 Combine flour, oil and salt in work bowl of food processor. Process 5 seconds or until mixed. Add yeast mixture and 1 egg; process 10 seconds or until blended.

3 Turn on processor and slowly drizzle just enough remaining warm water through feed tube so dough forms a ball that cleans side of bowl. Process until ball turns around bowl about 25 times. Turn off processor and let dough stand 1 to 2 minutes.

4 Turn on processor and gradually drizzle in enough remaining warm water to make dough soft, smooth and satiny but not sticky. Process until dough turns around bowl about 15 times.

5 Shape dough into ball. Place in greased bowl; turn to grease top. Cover and let stand about 15 minutes.

6 Divide dough into 12 equal pieces. Shape each piece into 6-inch-long rope. Bring ends together to form doughnut shape. Moisten ends and pinch together to seal. Place bagels on greased baking sheet and let stand at room temperature about 15 minutes.

7 Bring 2 quarts water and remaining 2 tablespoons sugar to a boil in Dutch oven or stockpot. Working in batches, gently place bagels in boiling water. When they rise to the surface, turn and cook 1½ to 2 minutes until puffy. Remove bagels with slotted spoon to greased baking sheet.

8 Preheat oven to 425°F. Whisk remaining egg and 2 tablespoons cold water in small bowl; brush over bagels. Bake 20 to 25 minutes or until crusts are golden and crisp. Remove to wire rack to cool.

KitchenAid

appetizers and small plates

Samosas

• • •

2¼ cups plus 3 tablespoons all-purpose flour, divided

½ teaspoon salt

4 tablespoons vegetable oil plus additional for frying, divided

¾ cup warm water

2 large potatoes

1 bunch green onions, trimmed and chopped

2 fresh green chiles, seeded and minced (optional)

½ cup fresh cilantro, chopped

1 teaspoon whole cumin seeds

2 teaspoons curry powder

½ teaspoon salt

Tamarind Sauce (recipe follows)

MAKES 16 SAMOSAS

1 Combine 2¼ cups flour and salt in bowl of stand mixer; attach whisk. Whisk on low 5 seconds to combine. Add 2 tablespoons oil; mix until mixture resembles fine bread crumbs. Replace whisk with flat beater. Add warm water. Mix on low 45 seconds or until dough just comes together. Add remaining 3 tablespoons flour; mix on low 4 minutes or until smooth and elastic. Shape dough into ball. Place in greased bowl. Cover and let stand 30 to 40 minutes.

2 Meanwhile, place potatoes in large saucepan; cover with cold water. Bring to a boil. Reduce heat; simmer, covered, 20 minutes or until tender. Drain and let stand until cool enough to handle. Peel and dice potatoes into ½-inch pieces.

3 Heat 2 tablespoons oil in large skillet over medium-high heat. Add onions; sauté 45 seconds. Add potatoes, chiles, if desired, cilantro, cumin seeds, curry powder and salt; sauté 1 minute or until fragrant. Set aside to cool.

4 Divide dough into 16 equal pieces; roll into balls. Roll balls into 4-inch circles on floured surface with floured rolling pin. Place 2 heaping teaspoons potato mixture in center of each circle. Lift one side of dough circle; crease in the middle. Lift opposite side of dough; pinch edges together. Fold up bottom end and pinch closed to form a triangle. Place samosas on baking sheet; refrigerate 1 hour. Prepare Tamarind Sauce.

5 Heat 2 inches of oil in large deep skillet over medium heat to 360°F. Working in batches, fry samosas 1 to 2 minutes per side until golden brown (return oil to 360°F between batches). Drain on paper towels. Serve warm with Tamarind Sauce.

Tamarind Sauce

MAKES 2 CUPS

  2 **cups water**

  ⅓ **cup sugar**

  2 **tablespoons tamarind paste**

Combine all ingredients in medium saucepan. Bring to a boil over medium heat. Reduce heat to low; simmer until reduced by two-thirds.

Arancini

• • •

Risotto alla Milanese (recipe follows)

1½ cups Italian seasoned dry bread crumbs

3 egg whites

12 (½-inch) pieces fresh mozzarella

12 (½-inch) pieces fresh Parmigiano Reggiano cheese

12 (¼-inch) cubes ham

2 cups canola oil

MAKES 12 SMALL ARANCINI

1 Prepare Risotto alla Milanese. Spread on nonstick baking sheet; cool completely. Spread bread crumbs on plate. Beat egg whites in small bowl.

2 Line baking sheet with waxed paper. Working with 2 tablespoons risotto at a time, flatten into 3-inch disc. Place one piece each of mozzarella cheese, Parmigiano Reggiano cheese and ham in center of disc. Fold edges up to cover filling, gently pinching seams to seal. Roll between palms to form ball roughly the size of a large egg.

3 Coat with bread crumbs, then egg whites, then again with bread crumbs. Place on prepared baking sheet. Repeat with remaining ingredients. Cover and refrigerate 1 hour or overnight.

4 Heat oil in large deep skillet to 360°F. Cook 1 minute per side or until golden brown. Transfer to wire rack. Serve warm.

Risotto alla Milanese

MAKES 4 SERVINGS

4 cups chicken or vegetable broth

2 tablespoons butter

2 tablespoons olive oil

1 shallot, minced

1 cup arborio rice

¼ cup white wine

1 generous pinch saffron threads, ground to a powder

¼ cup grated Parmesan cheese

Salt and freshly ground black pepper

1 Bring broth to a simmer in medium saucepan over medium-high heat; keep warm over low heat.

2 Heat butter and oil in large saucepan over medium-high heat. Add shallot; sauté 30 seconds or just until beginning to brown.

3 Add rice; sauté 1 to 2 minutes or until edges of rice become translucent. Add wine and saffron; sauté until wine evaporates.

4 Reduce heat to medium-low. Add ½ cup broth, stirring constantly until broth is absorbed. Repeat until all broth is used. Stir in Parmesan cheese. Season with salt and pepper.

Mushroom-Onion **Tartlets**

• • •

4 ounces cream cheese

3 tablespoons butter, divided

¾ cup plus 1 teaspoon all-purpose flour, divided

8 ounces fresh mushrooms, coarsely chopped

½ cup chopped green onions

1 egg

¼ cup dried thyme

½ cup (2 ounces) shredded Swiss cheese

MAKES 24 TARTLETS

1 Combine cream cheese and 2 tablespoons butter in bowl of stand mixer. Beat on medium about 1 minute. Stop and scrape bowl. Add ¾ cup flour; mix on low about 1 minute or until well blended. Shape dough into ball. Wrap in waxed paper or plastic wrap; refrigerate 1 hour.

2 Meanwhile, melt remaining 1 tablespoon butter in medium skillet over medium heat. Add mushrooms and onions; sauté 6 to 8 minutes or until mushrooms are tender. Cool slightly.

3 Preheat oven to 375°F. Spray 24 mini (1¾-inch) muffin pan cups with nonstick cooking spray. Divide dough into 24 pieces. Press each piece into muffin cup. Return to refrigerator while preparing filling.

4 Combine egg, thyme and remaining 1 teaspoon flour in mixer bowl. Beat on medium-high about 30 seconds. Stir in Swiss cheese and mushroom mixture on low. Divide filling among prepared muffin cups.

5 Bake 15 to 20 minutes or until egg mixture is puffed and golden brown. Carefully remove from pan. Serve warm.

KitchenAid

Meatball **Hors d'Oeuvres**

• • •

Tangy Barbecue Sauce
(recipe follows)

1 pound ground beef

⅓ cup dry bread crumbs

⅓ cup grated Parmesan cheese

2 egg yolks

2 tablespoons chopped fresh parsley

2 tablespoons chopped
stuffed olives

¾ teaspoon garlic salt

½ teaspoon dried oregano

¼ teaspoon freshly ground black pepper

¼ cup olive oil

MAKES 30 MEATBALLS

1 Prepare Tangy Barbecue Sauce; keep warm.

2 Combine ground beef, bread crumbs, Parmesan cheese, egg yolks, parsley, olives, garlic salt, oregano and pepper in bowl of stand mixer; mix on low 1 minute. Shape mixture into 30 (1-inch) balls.

3 Heat olive oil in large skillet over medium-high heat. Add meatballs; sauté until well browned and cooked through. Drain on paper towels. Transfer meatballs to serving dish; add barbecue sauce and stir to coat. Serve warm.

Tangy Barbecue Sauce

MAKES 2 CUPS

1¼ cups packed brown sugar

1 cup ketchup

1 cup strong brewed coffee

½ cup finely chopped onion

2 tablespoons Worcestershire sauce

2 tablespoons vinegar

1 teaspoon salt

⅛ teaspoon freshly ground black pepper

Combine all ingredients in medium saucepan. Cook over medium heat 10 minutes, stirring occasionally. Reduce heat; simmer 30 minutes.

Onion and **White Bean Spread**

• • •

1 can (about 15 ounces) cannellini or Great Northern beans, rinsed and drained

¼ cup chopped green onions

¼ cup grated Parmesan cheese

¼ cup olive oil, plus additional for serving

1 tablespoon fresh rosemary leaves, chopped

2 cloves garlic, minced

French bread slices, toasted

MAKES 1¼ CUPS SPREAD

1 Combine beans, green onions, Parmesan, ¼ cup olive oil, rosemary and garlic in food processor; process 30 to 40 seconds or until mixture is almost smooth.

2 Transfer to serving bowl. Drizzle with additional olive oil just before serving. Serve with bread.

○ **TIP**

FOR A MORE RUSTIC-LOOKING SPREAD, COMBINE ALL INGREDIENTS IN A MEDIUM BOWL AND MASH WITH A POTATO MASHER.

Goat Cheese-**Stuffed Figs**

● ● ●

7 fresh firm ripe figs

7 slices prosciutto

1 package (4 ounces) goat cheese

Freshly ground black pepper

MAKES 4 TO 6 SERVINGS

1 Preheat broiler. Line small baking sheet with foil. Cut figs in half vertically. Cut prosciutto slices in half to make 14 (4×1-inch) pieces.

2 Scoop 1 teaspoon goat cheese onto cut side of each fig half. Wrap prosciutto slice around fig and goat cheese. Sprinkle with pepper.

3 Broil about 4 minutes or until cheese softens and figs are heated through.

Beef **Empanadas**

• • •

1 tablespoon olive oil

3 tablespoons finely chopped onion

1 clove garlic, minced

¼ pound lean ground beef

2 tablespoons chopped pimiento-stuffed green olives

2 tablespoons raisins

2 tablespoons ketchup

1 tablespoon chopped fresh parsley

½ teaspoon ground cumin

½ (17-ounce) package puff pastry (1 sheet), thawed

1 egg yolk

MAKES 4 SERVINGS

1 Preheat oven to 400°F. Line baking sheet with parchment paper.

2 Heat oil in large skillet over medium-high heat. Add onion and garlic; sauté 2 to 3 minutes. Add beef; cook 6 to 8 minutes or until browned, stirring to separate meat. Drain fat. Add olives, raisins, ketchup, parsley and cumin; sauté 1 to 2 minutes.

3 Roll out pastry into 12-inch square on lightly floured surface. Cut into nine 4-inch squares. Place 1 rounded tablespoonful beef mixture in center of each square. Fold over to form triangle; seal edges with fork. Place on prepared baking sheet. Bake 18 to 20 minutes or until golden brown.

Mini **Smoked Salmon Latkes**

● ● ●

2 cups frozen shredded hash brown
potatoes, thawed and drained

1 egg, lightly beaten

2 tablespoons finely chopped shallot

1 tablespoon all-purpose flour

1 tablespoon heavy cream

½ teaspoon salt

¼ teaspoon freshly ground black pepper

1 tablespoon butter, divided

1 tablespoon vegetable oil, divided

1 package (4 ounces) smoked salmon

Sour cream

Black whitefish caviar (optional)

MAKES 24 APPETIZERS

1 Chop potatoes into smaller pieces. Combine potatoes, egg, shallot, flour, cream, salt and pepper in large bowl; mix well.

2 Heat half each of butter and oil in large nonstick skillet over medium-high heat. Spoon tablespoonfuls of potato mixture into skillet; flatten with spatula to make small pancakes. Cook about 3 minutes per side or until golden. Remove to plate. Repeat with remaining butter, oil and potato mixture.

3 Cut salmon into 24 pieces. Top each pancake with piece of salmon, tiny dollop of sour cream and pinch of caviar, if desired. Serve immediately.

Citrus-Marinated Olives

• • •

1 cup (about 8 ounces) large green
olives, drained

1 cup kalamata olives, rinsed
and drained

⅓ cup extra virgin olive oil

¼ cup orange juice

3 tablespoons sherry vinegar
or red wine vinegar

2 tablespoons lemon juice

1 tablespoon grated orange peel

1 tablespoon grated lemon peel

½ teaspoon ground cumin

¼ teaspoon red pepper flakes

MAKES 2 CUPS

Combine all ingredients in jar or medium glass bowl. Cover and marinate at room temperature overnight. Refrigerate up to 2 weeks.

Tiropetas

• • •

½ pound feta cheese, drained and crumbled

3 ounces cream cheese

½ cup cottage cheese

¼ cup grated Romano cheese

⅛ teaspoon freshly ground pepper

Dash nutmeg

2 eggs

1 package (16 ounces) phyllo dough, thawed

1 cup (2 sticks) butter, melted

MAKES 4 DOZEN APPETIZERS

1 Preheat oven to 350°F. Place feta cheese, cream cheese and cottage cheese in bowl of stand mixer. Beat on medium 1 minute or until fluffy. Stop and scrape bowl. Add Romano cheese, pepper and nutmeg; mix on low 30 seconds. Add eggs, one at a time, beating on low 30 seconds after each addition. Increase speed to medium and beat 15 seconds.

2 Place one sheet of phyllo dough on a flat surface. Cover remaining phyllo dough with a slightly damp towel. Brush sheet with butter, top with another sheet and brush again with butter. Cut lengthwise into 2½-inch-wide strips. Place 1 teaspoon cheese mixture on bottom corner of strip. Fold over into a triangle shape and continue folding like a flag. Brush with butter and place on greased baking sheet. Repeat with remaining phyllo dough and cheese mixture. Work quickly as phyllo dough dries out quickly.

3 Bake 15 to 20 minutes or until golden brown. Serve immediately.

Garden **Ratatouille**

● ● ●

2 tablespoons extra virgin olive oil

1 cup chopped sweet onion

1 yellow or red bell pepper, cut into ½-inch cubes

4 cloves garlic, minced

1 medium eggplant (about 12 ounces), peeled and cut into ½-inch cubes

1 can (about 14 ounces) Italian-style stewed tomatoes, coarsely chopped

⅓ cup sliced pitted kalamata or black olives

1 tablespoon plus 1½ teaspoons balsamic vinegar

½ teaspoon salt

¼ teaspoon red pepper flakes

¼ cup chopped fresh basil

8 slices French bread, toasted

MAKES 8 SERVINGS

1 Heat oil in large deep skillet over medium heat. Add onion; sauté 5 minutes. Add bell pepper and garlic; sauté 5 minutes. Stir in eggplant, tomatoes and olives. Bring to a boil over high heat. Reduce heat; simmer, covered, 15 minutes or until vegetables are tender.

2 Stir in vinegar, salt and red pepper flakes; cook, uncovered, 2 minutes. Remove from heat; stir in basil. Serve warm or at room temperature on bread.

Margherita **Panini Bites**

● ● ●

1 loaf (16 ounces) ciabatta or crusty
Italian bread, cut into 16 (½-inch) slices

8 teaspoons pesto

16 fresh basil leaves

8 slices mozzarella cheese

24 thin plum tomato slices (about
3 tomatoes)

Olive oil

MAKES 32 PANINI BITES

1 Preheat grill or broiler. Spread one side of eight bread slices with
1 teaspoon pesto. Top with 2 basil leaves, 1 cheese slice and 3 tomato slices.
Top with remaining bread slices.

2 Brush outsides of sandwiches lightly with oil. Grill sandwiches 5 minutes
or until lightly browned and cheese is melted.

3 Cut each sandwich into four pieces. Serve warm.

NOTE: Panini bites can also be cooked in a panini press, grill pan or large
skillet. Press down sandwiches with a heavy skillet while they cook using a
grill pan or skillet.

Olive **Tapenade**

● ● ●

1 can (6 ounces) medium
pitted black olives

½ cup pimiento-stuffed
green olives

1 tablespoon roasted garlic*

½ teaspoon dry mustard

½ cup (2 ounces) crumbled
feta cheese

1 tablespoon olive oil

Sliced French bread, toasted

*To roast garlic, preheat oven to 400°F.
Remove outer layers of papery skin and
cut ¼ inch off top of garlic head. Place
cut side up on a piece of heavy-duty foil.
Drizzle with 2 teaspoons olive oil; wrap
tightly in foil. Bake 25 to 30 minutes or
until cloves feel soft when pressed. Cool
slightly before squeezing out garlic pulp.

MAKES 1³/₄ CUPS TAPENADE

1 Combine olives, roasted garlic and mustard in food processor or blender; process until finely chopped.

2 Combine olive mixture, feta cheese and oil in medium bowl; stir until well blended. Serve with bread.

Thai **Chicken Wings**

• • •

1 tablespoon peanut oil

5 pounds chicken wings, tips removed and split at the joint

½ cup coconut milk

1 tablespoon Thai green curry paste

1 tablespoon fish sauce*

1 tablespoon sugar

¾ cup prepared spicy peanut sauce*

Both fish sauce and spicy peanut sauce can be found in the Asian section of well-stocked supermarkets.

MAKES 8 SERVINGS

1 Heat oil in large nonstick skillet over medium-high heat. Brown chicken wings in batches about 6 minutes. Transfer wings to 3½- to 4-quart slow cooker.

2 Stir in coconut milk, curry paste, fish sauce and sugar. Cover; cook on LOW 6 to 7 hours or on HIGH 3 to 3½ hours or until cooked through. Drain cooking liquid. Stir in peanut sauce before serving.

Mini **Carnitas Tacos**

• • •

1½ pounds boneless pork loin, cut into 1-inch cubes

1 onion, finely chopped

½ cup reduced-sodium chicken broth

1 tablespoon chili powder

2 teaspoons ground cumin

1 teaspoon dried oregano

½ teaspoon minced canned chipotle chile in adobo sauce

½ cup pico de gallo

2 tablespoons chopped fresh cilantro

½ teaspoon salt

12 (6-inch) flour or corn tortillas

¾ cup (3 ounces) shredded sharp Cheddar cheese

3 tablespoons sour cream

MAKES 36 CARNITAS

1 Combine pork, onion, broth, chili powder, cumin, oregano and chipotle in 3½- to 4-quart slow cooker. Cover; cook on LOW 6 hours or on HIGH 3 hours or until pork is very tender. Pour off cooking liquid.

2 Remove pork to cutting board; shred with two forks. Return to slow cooker; stir in pico de gallo, cilantro and salt. Cover and keep warm.

3 Cut three circles from each tortilla with 2-inch biscuit cutter. Top with pork, Cheddar cheese and sour cream. Serve warm.

KitchenAid

Sweet and Spicy **Beer Nuts**

• • •

2 cups pecan halves

2 teaspoons salt

2 teaspoons chili powder

2 teaspoons olive oil

½ teaspoon ground cumin

¼ teaspoon ground red pepper

½ cup sugar

½ cup beer

MAKES 3 CUPS

1 Preheat oven to 350°F. Line baking sheet with foil.

2 Mix pecans, salt, chili powder, olive oil, cumin and red pepper in small bowl. Spread on prepared baking sheet. Bake 10 minutes or until fragrant. Cool on baking sheet on wire rack.

3 Combine sugar and beer in medium saucepan. Heat over medium-high heat until mixture registers 250°F on candy thermometer. Remove from heat; carefully stir in nuts and any loose spices. Spread sugared nuts on same baking sheet, separating clusters. Cool completely. Break up any large pieces before serving.

soups and stews

Spicy African **Chickpea** and **Sweet Potato Stew**

• • •

Spice Paste (recipe follows)

1½ pounds sweet potatoes, peeled and cubed

2 cups vegetable broth or water

1 can (16 ounces) whole plum tomatoes, undrained, chopped

1 can (16 ounces) chickpeas, rinsed and drained

1½ cups sliced fresh okra *or* 1 package (10 ounces) frozen cut okra, thawed

Yellow Couscous (recipe follows)

Hot pepper sauce

MAKES 4 SERVINGS

1 Prepare Spice Paste.

2 Combine sweet potatoes, broth, tomatoes with juice, chickpeas, okra and Spice Paste in large saucepan. Bring to a boil over high heat. Reduce heat to low; simmer, covered, 15 minutes. Uncover; simmer 10 minutes or until vegetables are tender.

3 Meanwhile, prepare Yellow Couscous. Serve stew over couscous with hot pepper sauce.

Spice Paste

6   cloves garlic, peeled

1   teaspoon coarse salt

2   teaspoons sweet paprika

1½ teaspoons cumin seeds

1   teaspoon cracked black pepper

½   teaspoon ground ginger

½   teaspoon ground allspice

1   tablespoon olive oil

1 Combine garlic and salt in blender or small food processor; process until garlic is finely chopped. Add paprika, cumin seeds, black pepper, ginger and allspice; process 15 seconds.

2 With motor running, through cover opening; process until mixture forms paste.

Yellow Couscous

1 tablespoon olive oil

5 green onions, sliced

1²/₃ cups water

⅛ teaspoon saffron threads *or* ½ teaspoon ground turmeric

¼ teaspoon salt

1 cup uncooked couscous

MAKES 3 CUPS

Heat oil in medium saucepan over medium heat. Add onions; sauté 4 minutes. Add water, saffron and salt. Bring to a boil. Stir in couscous. Remove from heat. Cover; let stand 5 minutes.

KitchenAid

Cream of **Asparagus Soup**

● ● ●

1 pound asparagus

3½ cups vegetable broth, divided

¼ cup (½ stick) butter

¼ cup all-purpose flour

½ cup light cream or half-and-half

½ teaspoon salt

⅛ teaspoon freshly ground black pepper

MAKES 6 TO 8 SERVINGS

1 Trim off and discard tough ends of asparagus. Cut asparagus into 1-inch pieces. Bring 1 cup broth to a simmer in medium saucepan over medium heat. Add asparagus; cook 5 to 7 minutes or until tender.

2 Remove 1 cup asparagus pieces; set aside. Place remaining asparagus pieces with broth in blender or food processor; blend until smooth.

3 Melt butter in large saucepan. Whisk in flour until smooth; cook 1 minute, whisking constantly. Gradually whisk in remaining 2½ cups broth; cook until slightly thickened, stirring occasionally. Stir in cream, salt, pepper, asparagus purée and reserved asparagus pieces; cook until heated through.

Spicy Thai **Coconut Soup**

• • •

2 cups chicken broth

1 can (13½ ounces) light coconut milk

1 tablespoon minced fresh ginger

½ to 1 teaspoon red curry paste

3 cups coarsely shredded cooked chicken (about 12 ounces)

1 can (15 ounces) straw mushrooms, drained

1 can (8¾ ounces) baby corn, drained

2 tablespoons lime juice

¼ cup chopped fresh cilantro

MAKES 4 SERVINGS

Whisk broth, coconut milk, ginger and red curry paste in large saucepan until well blended. Add chicken, mushrooms and corn. Bring to a simmer over medium heat; cook until heated through. Stir in lime juice. Sprinkle with cilantro before serving.

NOTE: Red curry paste can be found in jars in the Asian section of well-stocked supermarkets. Spice levels vary among brands so start with ½ teaspoon, then add more as desired.

Tomato Soup

• • •

1 tablespoon vegetable oil

1 cup chopped onion

2 cloves garlic, coarsely chopped

½ cup chopped carrot

¼ cup chopped celery

2 cans (28 ounces each) crushed tomatoes in purée

3½ cups vegetable or chicken broth

1 tablespoon Worcestershire sauce

½ to 1 teaspoon salt

½ teaspoon dried thyme

¼ to ½ teaspoon freshly ground black pepper

2 to 4 drops hot pepper sauce

MAKES 6 SERVINGS

1 Heat oil in large saucepan over medium-high heat. Add onion and garlic; sauté 1 to 2 minutes or until onion is soft. Add carrot and celery; cook 7 to 9 minutes or until tender, stirring frequently.

2 Stir in tomatoes, broth, Worcestershire sauce, salt, thyme, black pepper and hot pepper sauce. Reduce heat to low; simmer, covered, 20 minutes, stirring frequently.

3 For smoother soup, remove from heat. Let cool about 10 minutes. Blend soup with immersion blender or purée in batches in blender or food processor. Return soup to saucepan; simmer 3 to 5 minutes or until heated through.

Miso Soup with Tofu

• • •

½ cup dried bonito flakes*

4 cups vegetable or chicken broth

2 teaspoons vegetable oil

1 leek, finely chopped

1 tablespoon white miso

8 ounces firm tofu, cut into ½-inch cubes (about 1½ cups)

*Dried bonito flakes (katsuobushi) are available in the Asian section of well-stocked supermarkets or in Asian stores. If unavailable, add an additional 1 tablespoon miso.

MAKES 4 SERVINGS

1 Combine bonito flakes and broth in medium saucepan. Bring to a boil. Strain through fine-mesh sieve; reserve broth.

2 Heat oil in medium saucepan over medium heat. Add leek; sauté 2 to 3 minutes or until tender. Return broth to saucepan. Add miso; stir well. Reduce heat to low. Add tofu; cook until heated through.

Oven-Roasted **Onion Soup**

• • •

¼ cup (½ stick) butter

3 large yellow onions, thinly sliced

1 teaspoon salt

½ teaspoon freshly ground pepper

6 cups reduced-sodium beef broth

½ cup brewed coffee

¼ cup dry sherry

1 baguette, cut into ½-inch slices

1 cup (4 ounces) shredded Swiss cheese

MAKES 4 SERVINGS

1 Preheat oven to 325°F. Melt butter in Dutch oven over medium heat. Add onions, salt and pepper; sauté about 10 minutes or until onions are golden but not browned. Cover and bake 45 minutes, stirring once.

2 Stir in broth; cover and bake 30 minutes. Remove from oven; stir in coffee and sherry. Bring soup to a simmer over medium heat. Remove from heat.

3 Place bread slices on baking sheet. Bake until lightly browned on both sides, turning once.

4 Preheat broiler. Ladle soup into four ovenproof bowls; top each serving with 2 to 3 slices of toast and ¼ cup Swiss cheese.

5 Place bowls in large baking pan; broil 2 to 3 minutes or until cheese is melted and bubbly.

Cordero Stew with Cornmeal Dumplings

• • •

2 pounds lean lamb stew meat with bones, cut into 2-inch pieces *or* 1½ pounds lean boneless lamb, cut into 1½-inch cubes

1 teaspoon salt

½ teaspoon freshly ground black pepper

2½ tablespoons vegetable oil, divided

1 large onion, chopped

1 clove garlic, minced

2 tablespoons tomato paste

2 teaspoons chili powder

1 teaspoon ground coriander

4 cups water

3 small potatoes, cut into 1½-inch chunks

2 large carrots, cut into 1-inch pieces

1 package (10 ounces) frozen corn

⅓ cup coarsely chopped celery leaves

CORNMEAL DUMPLINGS

½ cup all-purpose flour

½ cup yellow cornmeal

1 teaspoon baking powder

¼ teaspoon salt

2½ tablespoons cold butter

½ cup milk

MAKES 6 SERVINGS

1 For stew, sprinkle meat with salt and pepper. Heat 2 tablespoons oil in large saucepan over medium-high heat. Brown lamb on all sides in batches; transfer to medium bowl.

2 Heat remaining ½ tablespoon oil in same saucepan over medium heat. Add onion and garlic; sauté until onion is tender. Stir in tomato paste, chili powder, coriander and water. Add lamb, potatoes, carrots, corn and chopped celery leaves. Bring to a boil. Reduce heat; cover and simmer 1 hour 15 minutes or until lamb is tender.

3 During last 15 minutes of cooking, prepare dumplings. Combine flour, cornmeal, baking powder and salt in medium bowl. Cut in butter with pastry blender until mixture resembles coarse crumbs. Make well in center; add milk and stir with fork until dough forms.

4 Drop six dollops of dough onto stew. Cover and simmer 18 minutes or until dumplings are firm to the touch and toothpick inserted into centers comes out clean.

Matzo Ball Soup

● ● ●

4 eggs

1 cup matzo meal

¼ cup (½ stick) butter, melted and cooled

2 tablespoons water

1 tablespoon grated onion

½ teaspoon salt

⅛ teaspoon white pepper *or* ¼ teaspoon freshly ground black pepper

2 quarts chicken broth

Chopped fresh parsley (optional)

MAKES 6 SERVINGS

1 Place eggs in bowl of stand mixer. Beat on medium until blended. Add matzo meal, butter, 2 tablespoons water, onion, salt and pepper; mix on low until well blended. Let stand 15 to 30 minutes. With wet hands, shape mixture into 12 (2-inch) balls. Bring 8 cups water to a boil in large saucepan. Drop matzo balls, one at a time, into boiling water. Reduce heat. Cover; simmer 35 to 40 minutes or until matzo balls are cooked through. Remove from saucepan with slotted spoon; drain. Discard water.

2 Bring broth to a boil in same saucepan over high heat. Add matzo balls. Reduce heat; cover and simmer 5 minutes or until matzo balls are heated through. Garnish with parsley.

KitchenAid

Tortilla Soup

• • •

3 (6-inch) corn tortillas

2 teaspoons vegetable oil, plus additional for frying

½ cup chopped onion

1 small clove garlic, minced

2 cans (about 14 ounces each) chicken broth

1 can (about 14 ounces) whole tomatoes, undrained, chopped

1 cup shredded cooked chicken

2 teaspoons lime juice

1 small avocado, diced

2 tablespoons chopped fresh cilantro

MAKES 4 SERVINGS

1 Cut tortillas in half, then cut crosswise into ½-inch strips. Pour oil to depth of ½ inch in small saucepan. Heat over medium-high heat until oil reaches 360°F. Cook tortilla strips in batches 1 minute or until crisp and lightly browned. Remove with slotted spoon; drain on paper towels.

2 Heat 2 teaspoons oil in medium saucepan over medium heat. Add onion and garlic; sauté until onion is soft. Add broth and tomatoes with juice. Bring to a boil. Reduce heat; cover and simmer 15 minutes. Add chicken and lime juice. Simmer 5 minutes.

3 Ladle soup into bowls; top with avocado, tortilla strips and cilantro.

Greek-Style **Chicken Stew**

• • •

3 pounds skinless chicken breasts

All-purpose flour

2 tablespoons olive oil, divided

2 cups cubed peeled eggplant

2 cups sliced mushrooms

¾ cup coarsely chopped onion

2 cloves garlic, minced

1 teaspoon dried oregano

½ teaspoon dried basil

½ teaspoon dried thyme

2 cups reduced-sodium chicken broth

¼ cup dry sherry

¼ teaspoon salt

¼ teaspoon freshly ground black pepper

1 can (14 ounces) artichoke hearts, drained

3 cups hot cooked wide egg noodles

MAKES 6 SERVINGS

1 Coat chicken very lightly with flour. Heat 1 tablespoon olive oil in large saucepan over medium heat. Cook chicken, in batches if necessary, 10 to 15 minutes or until browned on all sides. Remove chicken to plate; drain fat.

2 Heat remaining 1 tablespoon olive oil in same saucepan over medium heat. Add eggplant, mushrooms, onion, garlic, oregano, basil and thyme; sauté 5 minutes.

3 Return chicken to saucepan. Stir in broth, sherry, salt and pepper; bring to a boil. Reduce heat to low; simmer, covered, about 1 hour or until chicken is no longer pink in center, adding artichoke hearts during last 20 minutes of cooking. Serve over noodles.

KitchenAid

Cream of Broccoli Soup with Croutons

• • •

3 tablespoons butter, divided

3 cups French or rustic bread, cut into ½-inch cubes

1 tablespoon olive oil

¼ cup grated Parmesan cheese

1 large onion, chopped

8 cups (about 1½ pounds) chopped broccoli

3 cups vegetable broth

1 cup heavy cream or half-and-half

1½ teaspoons salt

½ teaspoon freshly ground black pepper

MAKES 8 SERVINGS

1 Preheat oven to 350°F. Melt 1 tablespoon butter in small saucepan. Combine bread cubes, olive oil and melted butter in large bowl; toss to coat. Add cheese; toss to combine. Spread on 15×10-inch jelly-roll pan. Bake 12 to 14 minutes or until golden brown, stirring after 8 minutes. Cool completely.

2 Melt remaining 2 tablespoons butter in large saucepan over medium heat. Add onion; sauté 5 minutes. Add broccoli and broth; cover and bring to a boil over high heat. Reduce heat; simmer, covered, 25 minutes or until broccoli is very tender. Cool 10 minutes.

3 Blend soup with immersion blender or purée in batches in blender or food processor. Return soup to saucepan; stir in cream, salt and pepper. Cook over low heat until heated through. Do not boil. Serve soup with croutons.

pasta

Tuscan Pasta

• • •

12 ounces uncooked rigatoni

2 tablespoons olive oil

½ cup chopped onion

2 cloves garlic, minced

8 plum tomatoes, coarsely chopped

1 can (8 ounces) tomato sauce

1 teaspoon chopped fresh basil

1 teaspoon chopped fresh oregano

1 teaspoon chopped fresh rosemary

½ teaspoon salt

½ teaspoon freshly ground black pepper

Shaved Parmesan cheese

MAKES 6 SERVINGS

1 Cook pasta according to package directions until al dente. Drain; cover and keep warm.

2 Heat olive oil in medium saucepan over medium heat. Add onion; sauté 4 minutes or until tender. Add garlic; cook 1 minute.

3 Stir in tomatoes, tomato sauce, basil, oregano, rosemary, salt and pepper; bring to a boil. Reduce heat; simmer 6 minutes or until desired consistency is reached, stirring occasionally. Serve sauce over pasta with cheese.

KitchenAid

Rice Noodles with Broccoli and Tofu

● ● ●

1 package (14 ounces) firm or
extra firm tofu

1 package (8 to 10 ounces)
wide rice noodles

2 tablespoons peanut oil

3 medium shallots, sliced

6 cloves garlic, minced

1 jalapeño pepper, minced

2 teaspoons minced fresh ginger

3 cups broccoli florets

3 tablespoons regular soy sauce

1 tablespoon sweet soy sauce*

1 to 2 tablespoons fish sauce

Fresh basil leaves (optional)

*If sweet soy sauce is unavailable, mix
3 teaspoons regular soy sauce with
1 teaspoon packed brown sugar in
small bowl until smooth.*

MAKES 4 TO 6 SERVINGS

1 Cut tofu crosswise in half. Place tofu on cutting board between layers of paper towels; place weighted saucepan or baking dish on top of tofu. Let stand 20 to 30 minutes. Place rice noodles in large bowl; cover with boiling water. Let stand 30 minutes or until softened.

2 Cut tofu into bite-size squares; blot dry. Heat oil in large skillet or wok over medium-high heat. Add tofu; stir-fry about 5 minutes or until tofu is lightly browned on all sides. Remove from skillet.

3 Add shallots, garlic, jalapeño and ginger to skillet; stir-fry 2 to 3 minutes. Add broccoli; stir-fry 1 minute. Cover and cook 3 minutes or until broccoli is crisp-tender.

4 Drain noodles, stir into skillet. Return tofu to skillet; add soy sauces and fish sauce. Stir-fry about 8 minutes or until noodles are coated and flavors are blended. Garnish with basil.

KitchenAid

Orecchiette with **Sausage and Broccoli Rabe**

• • •

1 tablespoon olive oil

1 pound mild Italian sausage

2 cloves garlic, minced

⅛ teaspoon red pepper flakes

1½ pounds broccoli rabe, stems trimmed, cut into 2-inch pieces

1 package (16 ounces) uncooked orecchiette pasta

¾ cup grated Parmesan cheese, plus additional for serving

Salt and freshly ground black pepper

MAKES 4 TO 6 SERVINGS

1 Bring large pot of salted water to a boil. Meanwhile, heat oil in large skillet over medium-high heat. Remove sausage from casings; add to skillet. Cook sausage about 8 minutes or until browned, stirring to break up meat. Add garlic and red pepper flakes; sauté 3 minutes.

2 Add broccoli rabe to boiling water; cook 2 minutes. Remove broccoli rabe with slotted spoon; transfer to skillet with sausage mixture. Cook over medium-low heat until crisp-tender, stirring occasionally.

3 Add pasta to boiling water; cook according to package directions. Drain pasta, reserving 1 cup cooking water. Combine pasta, sausage mixture and ¾ cup cheese in large serving bowl; mix well. Season with salt and black pepper. Add some of reserved cooking water if sauce is dry. Serve immediately with additional cheese, if desired.

Quick Pasta **Puttanesca**

• • •

1 package (16 ounces) uncooked dried spaghetti or linguine or Basic Egg Noodle Pasta (page 123), cut into spaghetti

3 tablespoons plus 1 teaspoon olive oil, divided

¼ to 1 teaspoon red pepper flakes*

1 tablespoon dried minced onion

1 teaspoon minced garlic

2 cans (6 ounces each) chunk light tuna packed in water, drained

1 can (28 ounces) diced tomatoes

1 can (8 ounces) tomato sauce

24 pitted kalamata or ripe olives

2 tablespoons capers, drained

For a mildly spicy dish, use ¼ teaspoon red pepper flakes. For a very spicy dish, use 1 teaspoon red pepper flakes.

MAKES 6 TO 8 SERVINGS

1 Cook spaghetti according to package directions; drain and return to saucepan. Add 1 teaspoon olive oil; toss to coat. Cover and keep warm.

2 Meanwhile, heat remaining 3 tablespoons olive oil in large skillet over medium-high heat. Add red pepper flakes; sauté until sizzling. Add onion and garlic; sauté 1 minute. Add tuna; sauté 2 to 3 minutes. Add tomatoes, tomato sauce, olives and capers. Cook, stirring frequently, until sauce is heated through.

3 Add sauce to spaghetti; mix well.

KitchenAid

Fettuccine with Asparagus and Lima Beans

• • •

8 ounces uncooked dried fettuccine or
Basic Egg Noodle Pasta (page 123),
cut into fettuccine

2 tablespoons butter

2 cups fresh asparagus pieces (about
1-inch long)

1 cup frozen lima beans, thawed

¼ teaspoon freshly ground black pepper

½ cup vegetable broth

1 cup half-and-half or heavy cream

1 cup grated Parmesan cheese

MAKES 4 SERVINGS

1 Cook fettuccine according to package directions. Drain; cover and keep warm.

2 Meanwhile, melt butter in large skillet over medium-high heat. Add asparagus, lima beans and black pepper; sauté 3 minutes. Add broth; simmer 3 minutes. Add half-and-half; simmer 3 to 4 minutes or until vegetables are tender.

3 Add vegetable mixture and cheese to fettuccine; toss well. Serve immediately.

Gemelli and **Grilled Summer Vegetables**

• • •

2 tablespoons pine nuts

1 clove garlic

1 cup loosely packed fresh basil leaves

3 tablespoons plus 1 teaspoon olive oil, divided

¼ cup grated Parmesan cheese

¼ teaspoon salt

¼ teaspoon freshly ground black pepper

2 large bell peppers (one each red and yellow)

12 stalks asparagus, trimmed

2 slices red onion

6 ounces (2¼ cups) uncooked gemelli or rotini pasta

1 cup grape or cherry tomatoes

MAKES 4 SERVINGS

1 Combine pine nuts and garlic in food processor; process until coarsely chopped. Add basil; process until finely chopped. With motor running, add 3 tablespoons olive oil. Stir in cheese, salt and black pepper. Set aside.

2 Prepare grill for direct cooking. Cut bell peppers in half; remove and discard seeds. Grill bell peppers, skin sides down, covered, over medium heat 10 to 12 minutes or until skins are blackened. Place peppers in paper or plastic bag; let stand 15 minutes. Remove and discard blackened skins. Cut peppers into chunks. Place in large bowl.

3 Toss asparagus and onion with remaining 1 teaspoon oil in medium bowl. Grill on covered grill over medium heat 8 to 10 minutes or until tender, turning once. Cut asparagus into 2-inch pieces and coarsely chop onion; add asparagus and onions to peppers.

4 Cook pasta according to package directions; drain and add to vegetables. Add basil mixture and tomatoes; toss to coat. Serve immediately.

Classic **Fettuccine Alfredo**

• • •

12 ounces uncooked dried fettuccine or Basic Egg Noodle Pasta (page 123), cut into fettuccine

²/₃ cup heavy cream

6 tablespoons unsalted butter

½ teaspoon salt

Generous dash white pepper

Generous dash ground nutmeg

1 cup grated Parmesan cheese

2 tablespoons chopped fresh parsley

MAKES 4 SERVINGS

1 Cook pasta according to package directions. Drain; cover and keep warm.

2 Meanwhile, heat cream and butter in large heavy skillet over medium-low heat until butter melts and mixture bubbles, stirring frequently. Sauté 2 minutes. Stir in salt, white pepper and nutmeg. Remove from heat. Gradually stir in cheese until well blended and smooth. Return to heat briefly to completely blend cheese, if necessary. (Do not let sauce bubble or cheese will become lumpy and tough.)

3 Pour sauce over pasta. Sauté over low heat 2 to 3 minutes or until sauce thickens and pasta is evenly coated. Sprinkle with chopped parsley. Serve immediately.

Fettuccine alla **Carbonara**

• • •

12 ounces uncooked dried fettuccine or Basic Egg Noodle Pasta (page 123), cut into fettuccine

4 ounces pancetta or bacon, cut crosswise into ½-inch-wide strips

3 cloves garlic, cut into halves

¼ cup dry white wine

⅓ cup heavy cream

1 egg

1 egg yolk

⅔ cup grated Parmesan cheese, divided

Dash white pepper

MAKES 4 SERVINGS

1 Cook fettuccine according to package directions. Drain; cover and keep warm.

2 Meanwhile, sauté pancetta and garlic in large skillet over medium-low heat 4 minutes or until pancetta is lightly browned. Reserve 2 tablespoons drippings in skillet with pancetta. Discard garlic and remaining drippings.

3 Add wine to pancetta mixture; cook over medium heat 3 minutes or until wine is almost evaporated. Add cream; sauté 2 minutes. Remove from heat.

4 Whisk egg and egg yolk in top of double boiler. Place top of double boiler over simmering water, adjusting heat to maintain simmer. Whisk ⅓ cup cheese and white pepper into egg mixture; cook until sauce thickens slightly, stirring constantly.

5 Pour pancetta mixture over fettuccine; toss to coat. Cook over medium-low heat until heated through. Add egg mixture; toss to coat. Serve with remaining ⅓ cup cheese.

KitchenAid

Bolognese Sauce

• • •

2 tablespoons olive oil

1½ pounds ground beef

½ pound ground pork

2 carrots, peeled and cut
into 1-inch pieces

2 stalks celery, cut into
1-inch pieces

1 large onion, cut into 8 wedges

¼ cup fresh parsley

3 cloves garlic

4 cups tomato purée*

¼ cup water

¼ cup dry red wine

2 tablespoons tomato paste

1½ teaspoons salt

1 teaspoon dried basil

1 teaspoon dried oregano

1 bay leaf

¼ teaspoon freshly ground
black pepper

Hot cooked fettuccine

Shredded Parmesan cheese

*Purée whole canned Italian plum
tomatoes with juice in food processor.
Or assemble Food Grinder with
Fruit/Vegetable Strainer; attach
to stand mixer. Strain 6 fresh plum
tomatoes into mixer bowl.

MAKES 2 QUARTS

1 Heat oil in 12-inch skillet over medium heat. Add beef, pork, carrots, celery, onion, parsley and garlic; sauté 20 minutes. Cool 10 minutes.

2 Process meat mixture in batches in food processor until coarsely ground.* Transfer mixture to large saucepan. Add tomato purée, water, wine, tomato paste, salt, basil, oregano, bay leaf and pepper. Bring to a simmer over medium-low heat; simmer, covered, 1 hour.

3 Serve sauce over pasta with cheese.

*Or assemble Food Grinder with coarse grinding plate; attach to stand mixer. Grind meat mixture into large bowl.

Pasta with **Creamy Vodka Sauce**

• • •

6 ounces uncooked campanelle
or bowtie pasta

1 tablespoon butter

3 plum tomatoes, seeded and chopped

2 cloves garlic, minced

3 tablespoons vodka

½ cup heavy cream

¼ teaspoon salt

¼ teaspoon red pepper flakes

⅓ cup grated Parmesan cheese

2 tablespoons chopped fresh chives

MAKES 4 SERVINGS

1 Cook pasta according to package directions. Drain; cover and keep warm.

2 Melt butter in large skillet over medium heat. Add tomatoes and garlic; cook 3 minutes, stirring frequently. Add vodka; simmer 2 minutes or until most of liquid has evaporated.

3 Stir in cream, salt and red pepper flakes; return to a simmer. Simmer 2 to 3 minutes or until slightly thickened. Remove from heat; let stand 2 minutes. Stir in cheese until melted.

4 Add sauce and chives to pasta; toss until pasta is coated. Serve immediately.

Lemon Salmon and Spinach Pasta

• • •

8 ounces uncooked dried fettuccine or
Basic Egg Noodle Pasta (page 123),
cut into fettuccine

¾ pound salmon fillet

4 teaspoons butter

2 cloves garlic, minced

1 teaspoon finely grated
lemon peel

¼ teaspoon red pepper flakes

2 tablespoons lemon juice

3 cups baby spinach leaves

½ cup shredded carrot

MAKES 4 SERVINGS

1 Cook fettuccine according to package directions. Drain; cover and keep warm.

2 Pat salmon dry with paper towels. Remove skin from salmon; discard. Cut fish into ½-inch pieces.

3 Meanwhile, melt butter in large skillet over medium-high heat. Add salmon, garlic, lemon peel and red pepper flakes; cook 4 to 7 minutes or until salmon flakes when tested with fork. Gently stir in lemon juice.

4 Add salmon mixture, spinach and carrot to hot cooked fettuccine; gently toss to combine. Serve immediately.

Spinach Pasta Pomodoro

● ● ●

3 tablespoons olive oil

3 cloves garlic, minced

3 cups tomato purée

½ cup chopped fresh basil

1 teaspoon *each* sugar and salt

¼ teaspoon freshly ground black pepper

1½ pounds fresh spinach fettuccine (page 123)

Shredded Parmesan cheese

*Purée whole canned Italian plum tomatoes with juice in food processor. Or assemble Food Grinder with Fruit/Vegetable Strainer; attach to stand mixer. Strain 6 fresh plum tomatoes into mixer bowl.

MAKES 6 SERVINGS

1 Heat olive oil in large saucepan over medium heat. Add garlic; sauté 2 minutes. Add tomato purée, basil, sugar, salt and pepper. Reduce heat; simmer, covered, 30 minutes.

2 Cook fettuccine according to package directions. Drain. Top with sauce and cheese.

Penne Pasta
with Chunky Tomato Sauce

• • •

1 package (8 ounces) unocooked
multigrain penne pasta

2 cups spicy marinara sauce

1 large ripe tomato, chopped (about
1½ cups)

4 cups packed baby spinach or torn
spinach leaves (4 ounces)

¼ cup grated Parmesan cheese

¼ cup chopped fresh basil

MAKES 8 SERVINGS

1 Cook pasta according to package directions. Drain; cover and keep warm.

2 Heat marinara sauce and tomato in medium saucepan over medium heat 3 to 4 minutes or until hot and bubbly, stirring occasionally. Remove from heat; stir in spinach.

3 Add tomato mixture to pasta; mix well. Serve with cheese and basil.

KitchenAid

Basic **Egg Noodle Pasta**

• • •

2¼ cups all-purpose flour

3 eggs

2 tablespoons water

1 tablespoon extra virgin olive oil

Variations:

For Semolina Pasta Dough, substitute 1¼ cups semolina flour and 1 cup all-purpose flour for the 2¼ cups all-purpose flour.

For Spinach Pasta Dough, omit water. Place 10 ounces thawed frozen spinach in food processor; pulse until very finely chopped. Squeeze dry. Add to dough with flour in step 1.

MAKES ABOUT 1 POUND

1 Place flour, eggs and water in bowl of stand mixer; beat on low 30 seconds. Replace flat beater with dough hook; knead on low 2 to 5 minutes or until dough is smooth. Shape dough into ball. Wrap in plastic wrap; let rest at room temperature 20 minutes or refrigerate until ready to use.

2 Cut dough into quarters. Flatten one piece of dough; dust with flour. Rewrap remaining pieces. Attach Pasta Sheet Roller to mixer and set to thickness setting 1. Turn mixer to medium speed; feed dough through rollers three or more times, folding and turning each time until smooth. If dough feels sticky, dust with flour. Change to setting 2 and feed dough sheet through rollers twice. Feed dough through once at settings 3 and 4; roll desired thickness. Let dough sheets rest on floured surface 10 minutes. Replace roller with desired Pasta Cutter. Feed dough sheets through cutter.

TO COOK PASTA: Add 1 tablespoon salt and 1 tablespoon oil to 6 quarts boiling water. Add pasta; cook 1 minute or until al dente, stirring frequently.

KitchenAid

beef and pork

Mustard Crusted **Rib Roast**

• • •

1 (3-rib) beef rib roast, trimmed* (6 to 7 pounds)

3 tablespoons Dijon mustard

1½ tablespoons chopped fresh tarragon or 1½ teaspoons dried tarragon

3 cloves garlic, minced

¼ cup dry red wine

⅓ cup finely chopped shallots

1 tablespoon all-purpose flour

1 cup beef broth

Ask your butcher to remove the chine bone for easier carving. Trim fat to ¼-inch thickness.

MAKES 6 TO 8 SERVINGS

1 Preheat oven to 450°F. Place roast, bone side down, in shallow roasting pan. Combine mustard, tarragon and garlic in small bowl; spread over top and sides of roast. Roast 10 minutes.

2 *Reduce oven temperature to 350°F.* Roast 2½ to 3 hours for medium or until internal temperature reaches 145°F when tested with meat thermometer inserted into thickest part of roast, not touching bone.

3 Transfer roast to cutting board; cover with foil. Let stand 10 to 15 minutes before carving. Internal temperature will continue to rise 5° to 10°F during stand time.

4 For gravy, reserve 1 tablespoon drippings from roasting pan; place in medium saucepan. Discard remaining drippings. Add wine to roasting pan; place over two burners. Cook over medium heat 2 minutes or until slightly thickened, stirring to scrape up browned bits.

5 Add shallots to drippings in saucepan; sauté over medium heat 4 minutes or until softened. Add flour; cook and stir 1 minute. Add broth and wine mixture; cook 5 minutes or until sauce thickens, stirring occasionally. Strain through fine-mesh sieve.

6 Carve roast into ½-inch-thick slices. Serve with gravy and mashed potatoes, if desired.

KitchenAid

Grilled Steak
with Arugula Salad

• • •

4 boneless beef top loin (strip) steaks,
¾ inch thick

1 cup balsamic or red wine
vinaigrette, divided

2 cups mixed salad greens

1½ cups baby arugula leaves

½ cup crumbled Gorgonzola cheese

MAKES 4 SERVINGS

1 Combine steaks and ½ cup vinaigrette in large resealable food storage bag. Seal bag; turn to coat. Marinate in refrigerator 20 to 30 minutes. Meanwhile, prepare grill for direct cooking.

2 Remove steaks from marinade; discard marinade. Grill steaks, covered, over medium-high heat 6 to 8 minutes for medium-rare (145°F) or until desired doneness, turning once.

3 Meanwhile, combine salad greens and arugula in medium bowl. Add remaining ½ cup vinaigrette; toss until well coated. Serve steaks with salad. Sprinkle with cheese.

KitchenAid

Beef Tenderloin
with Horseradish Cream

• • •

1 teaspoon chili powder

½ teaspoon salt, divided

¼ teaspoon plus ⅛ teaspoon freshly ground black pepper, divided

1 pound beef tenderloin

1 clove garlic, halved

2 teaspoons vegetable oil

⅓ cup sour cream

3 tablespoons milk

2 teaspoons mayonnaise

1 teaspoon prepared horseradish

¼ teaspoon dried rosemary

MAKES 4 SERVINGS

1 Preheat oven to 425°F. Combine chili powder, ¼ teaspoon salt and ¼ teaspoon pepper in small bowl. Rub tenderloin with garlic. Sprinkle seasoning mixture evenly over tenderloin.

2 Heat oil in medium ovenproof skillet over medium-high heat. Add tenderloin; cook 2 minutes on each side.

3 Place skillet in oven. Cook 30 minutes or until internal temperature of tenderloin reaches 140°F. Let stand 15 minutes.

4 Meanwhile, combine sour cream, milk, mayonnaise, horseradish, rosemary and remaining ¼ teaspoon salt and ⅛ teaspoon pepper in small bowl.

5 Slice tenderloin; serve with sauce.

Tuscan Beef

• • •

1 tablespoon olive oil

2 cloves garlic, minced

1½ teaspoons dried rosemary, divided

1 teaspoon salt

½ teaspoon freshly ground black pepper

4 beef ribeye or top loin (strip) steaks (8 to 10 ounces each), ¾- to 1 inch thick

¾ cup tomato-basil or marinara pasta sauce

½ cup sliced pimiento-stuffed green olives

1 tablespoon drained capers

MAKES 4 SERVINGS

1 Prepare grill for direct cooking or preheat broiler. Combine olive oil, garlic, 1 teaspoon rosemary, salt and pepper in small bowl; mix well. Spread mixture evenly over both sides of steaks.

2 Grill steaks, covered, over medium-high heat or broil 4 inches from heat 4 to 5 minutes per side for medium-rare (145°F) or to desired doneness.

3 Meanwhile, combine pasta sauce, olives, capers and remaining ½ teaspoon rosemary in small saucepan. Cook over medium heat until hot but not boiling. Transfer steaks to serving plates; top with sauce.

NOTE: The sodium content of prepared pasta sauces can vary widely. Since olives and capers both add salt, choose a pasta sauce with less sodium for best results.

Filet Mignon with Tarragon Butter

• • •

2 trimmed beef tenderloin steaks (8 ounces each), 1¼ to 1½ inches thick

2 teaspoons olive oil

¼ teaspoon kosher salt

⅛ teaspoon freshly ground black pepper

2 tablespoons butter

1 clove garlic, minced

2 teaspoons chopped fresh tarragon *or* ¾ teaspoon dried tarragon

MAKES 2 SERVINGS

1 Rub steaks with olive oil. Sprinkle with salt and pepper; let stand at room temperature 15 minutes.

2 Heat medium skillet over medium-high heat. Cook steaks 4 to 5 minutes on each side to 140°F for rare or to desired doneness. Transfer to serving plate; tent loosely with foil.

3 Melt butter in same skillet until it begins to brown slightly, scraping up any browned bits. Add garlic; cook about 15 seconds or until fragrant. Stir in tarragon. Pour sauce over steaks; serve immediately.

Grilled Strip Steaks with Fresh Chimichurri

• • •

Chimichurri (recipe follows)

4 bone-in strip steaks (8 ounces each), about 1 inch thick

¾ teaspoon ground cumin

¾ teaspoon salt

¼ teaspoon freshly ground black pepper

MAKES 4 SERVINGS

1 Prepare Chimichurri; set aside.

2 Oil grid. Prepare grill for direct cooking.

3 Sprinkle both sides of steaks with cumin, salt and pepper. Grill steaks over high heat 4 to 5 minutes on side for medium-rare (145°F), 5 to 7 minutes for medium.

4 Transfer steaks to serving plates; top with Chimichurri.

Chimichurri

½ cup packed fresh basil leaves

¼ cup packed fresh parsley

⅓ cup extra virgin olive oil

2 tablespoons packed fresh cilantro leaves

1 clove garlic

2 tablespoons fresh lemon juice

¼ teaspoon ground coriander

½ teaspoon grated orange peel

½ teaspoon salt

⅛ teaspoon freshly ground black pepper

Combine all ingredients in food processor or blender. Process until puréed, stopping to scrape side of bowl if necessary.

KitchenAid

Chinese **Peppercorn Beef**

● ● ●

2 teaspoons whole black
and pink peppercorns*

2 teaspoons coriander seeds

1 tablespoon peanut or canola oil

1 boneless beef top sirloin steak (1¼ to
1½ pounds) about 1¼ inches thick

2 teaspoons dark sesame oil

½ cup thinly sliced shallots
or sweet onion

½ cup chicken broth

2 tablespoons soy sauce

1 tablespoon dry sherry

1 tablespoon cold water

1 teaspoon cornstarch

2 tablespoons thinly sliced green onion
or chopped fresh cilantro

Or substitute all black peppercorns.

MAKES 4 SERVINGS

1 Place peppercorns and coriander seeds in small resealable food storage bag; seal bag. Coarsely crush spices using meat mallet or bottom of heavy saucepan. Brush peanut oil over both sides of steak; sprinkle with peppercorn mixture, pressing in lightly.

2 Heat large heavy skillet over medium-high heat. Add steak; cook 4 minutes without moving or until seared on bottom. Reduce heat to medium; turn steak and continue cooking 3 to 4 minutes for medium-rare (145°F) or until desired doneness. Transfer steak to cutting board; tent with foil.

3 Add sesame oil to same skillet; heat over medium heat. Add shallots; sauté 3 minutes, stirring frequently. Add broth, soy sauce and sherry; simmer 2 minutes.

4 Stir water into cornstarch in small bowl until smooth. Add to skillet; cook and stir 3 to 4 minutes or until sauce thickens. Carve steak crosswise into thin slices. Spoon sauce over steak; sprinkle with green onion.

KitchenAid

Beef Spiedini with Orzo

• • •

¼ cup olive oil

¼ cup dry red wine

2 cloves garlic, minced

1 teaspoon dried rosemary

1 teaspoon coarse salt, divided

½ teaspoon dried thyme

½ teaspoon freshly ground
black pepper

1½ pounds beef top sirloin steak, cut into
1-inch cubes

6 cups water

1 cup uncooked orzo

1 tablespoon butter

1 tablespoon chopped fresh parsley

MAKES 4 SERVINGS

1 Combine oil, wine, garlic, rosemary, ½ teaspoon salt, thyme and pepper in large resealable food storage bag. Add beef. Seal bag; turn to coat. Marinate in refrigerator 15 to 30 minutes.

2 Soak 8 (6- to 8-inch) wooden skewers in water 15 minutes. Prepare grill for direct cooking.

3 Bring 6 cups water and remaining ½ teaspoon salt to a boil in small saucepan over high heat. Add orzo; reduce heat and simmer 15 minutes or until tender. Drain. Stir in butter and parsley; keep warm.

4 Thread beef onto skewers. Grill over medium-high heat 8 to 10 minutes, turning occasionally. Serve with orzo.

Old-Fashioned Meat Loaf

• • •

1 teaspoon olive oil

1 cup finely chopped onion

4 cloves garlic, minced

1½ pounds ground beef

¾ cup old-fashioned oats

2 egg whites

1 cup chili sauce, divided

½ teaspoon freshly ground black pepper

¼ teaspoon salt

1 tablespoon Dijon mustard

MAKES 6 SERVINGS

1 Preheat oven to 375°F. Heat oil in large nonstick skillet over medium heat. Add onion; sauté 5 minutes. Add garlic; cook 1 minute. Remove from heat; transfer to large bowl. Let cool 5 minutes.

2 Add beef, oats, egg whites, ½ cup chili sauce, pepper and salt; mix well. Pack into 9×5-inch loaf pan. Combine remaining ½ cup chili sauce and mustard in small bowl; spoon evenly over top of meat loaf.

3 Bake 45 to 50 minutes or until internal temperature reaches 160°F. Let stand 5 minutes. Pour off any juices from pan. Cut into slices to serve.

KitchenAid

Veal Scallopini
with Exotic Mushrooms

• • •

½ pound veal cutlets

½ teaspoon salt, divided

¼ teaspoon freshly ground black pepper, divided

1 egg

1 tablespoon milk or water

½ cup dry bread crumbs

5 tablespoons butter, divided

2 tablespoons olive oil, divided

2 large shallots, chopped

8 ounces exotic mushrooms, such as cremini, oyster, baby bella and shiitake*

½ teaspoon herbes de Provence

½ cup chicken broth

2 lemon wedges (optional)

Exotic mushrooms make this dish special. However, you can substitute white button mushrooms, if you prefer.

MAKES 2 SERVINGS

1 Season veal with ¼ teaspoon salt and ⅛ teaspoon pepper. Whisk egg and milk in shallow dish. Place bread crumbs in second shallow dish. Coat veal with egg mixture; roll in bread crumbs to coat.

2 Heat 1 tablespoon butter and 1 tablespoon oil in large nonstick skillet over medium-high heat. Cook half of veal 3 minutes or until cooked through and golden brown, turning once. Transfer to plate and keep warm. Repeat with remaining 1 tablespoon butter, 1 tablespoon oil and veal.

3 Wipe out skillet with paper towels. Melt remaining 3 tablespoons butter in same skillet over medium-high heat. Add shallots; sauté 1 to 2 minutes or until translucent. Add mushrooms, remaining ¼ teaspoon salt, remaining ⅛ teaspoon pepper and herbes de Provence; sauté 3 to 4 minutes or until most of liquid evaporates. Add broth; cook 2 to 3 minutes or until slightly thickened.

4 Pour mushroom mixture over cutlets. Garnish with lemon wedges.

Sicilian **Steak Pinwheels**

● ● ●

¾ pound mild or hot Italian sausage, casings removed

1¾ cups fresh bread crumbs

¾ cup grated Parmesan cheese

2 eggs

3 tablespoons minced fresh parsley

1½ to 2 pounds round steak

1 cup frozen peas

1 cup pasta sauce

1 cup beef broth

MAKES 4 TO 6 SERVINGS

1 Coat 6-quart slow cooker with nonstick cooking spray. Mix sausage, bread crumbs, cheese, eggs and 3 tablespoons parsley in large bowl until well blended.

2 Place steak between sheets of plastic wrap; pound with tenderizer mallet or back of skillet until meat is about ⅜ inch thick. Remove top layer of plastic wrap. Spread sausage mixture over steak. Press peas into sausage mixture. Lift edge of plastic wrap at short end to begin rolling steak; roll up jelly-roll style. Tie at 2-inch intervals with kitchen string. Transfer to slow cooker.

3 Combine pasta sauce and broth in medium bowl. Pour over meat. Cover; cook on LOW 6 hours or until meat is tender and sausage is cooked through.

4 Transfer steak to serving platter. Let stand 20 minutes before removing string and slicing. Meanwhile, skim and discard excess fat from sauce. Serve steak slices with sauce.

KitchenAid

Cuban-Style **Marinated Skirt Steak**

● ● ●

2 pounds beef skirt steak,
cut into 6-inch pieces

2 cups orange juice, divided

½ cup lemon juice

½ cup lime juice

¼ cup olive oil

5 cloves garlic, minced

1 teaspoon dried oregano

1 large onion, halved
and thinly sliced

2 teaspoons grated orange peel, plus
additional for garnish

3 cups cooked white rice

3 cups cooked black beans

MAKES 6 SERVINGS

1 Place steaks in large resealable food storage bag. Mix 1 cup orange juice, lemon juice, lime juice, olive oil, garlic and oregano in small bowl; reserve ½ cup. Pour remaining juice mixture over steaks. Seal bag; turn to coat. Marinate in refrigerator 30 minutes.

2 Combine remaining 1 cup orange juice, onion and 2 teaspoons orange peel in separate small bowl; set aside.

3 Prepare grill for direct cooking. Remove steaks from marinade; discard marinade. Grill steaks, covered, over high heat 6 to 10 minutes or until desired doneness, turning once. Transfer to cutting board. Tent with foil; let stand 5 minutes before slicing.

4 Slice meat across the grain into thin slices. Transfer to serving platter. Remove onions from orange juice; arrange on top of meat. Sprinkle with reserved juice mixture and additional orange peel. Serve with rice and black beans.

Grilled Pork Chops
with Lager Barbecue Sauce

• • •

1 cup lager or other light-colored beer

⅓ cup maple syrup

3 tablespoons molasses

1 teaspoon Mexican-style
hot chile powder

4 bone-in center-cut pork chops
(2 to 2¼ pounds), 1 inch thick

Lager Barbecue Sauce (recipe follows)

¾ teaspoon salt

¼ teaspoon black pepper

MAKES 4 SERVINGS

1 Combine lager, maple syrup, molasses and chile powder in large resealable food storage bag; add pork. Seal bag; turn to coat. Marinate in refrigerator 2 hours, turning occasionally.

2 Prepare Lager Barbecue Sauce. Oil grid. Prepare grill for direct cooking.

3 Remove pork from marinade; discard marinade. Sprinkle pork with salt and pepper. Grill over medium-high heat 6 to 7 minutes on each side or until chops are well marked and thermometer inserted into center registers 145°F. Serve with Lager Barbecue Sauce.

Lager Barbecue Sauce

½   cup lager

⅓   cup ketchup

3   tablespoons maple syrup

2   tablespoons finely chopped onion

1   tablespoon molasses

1   tablespoon cider vinegar

½   teaspoon Mexican-style hot chile powder

Combine lager, ketchup, maple syrup, onion, molasses, vinegar and chile powder in small saucepan over medium heat. Bring to a gentle simmer and cook 10 to 12 minutes or until slightly thickened, stirring occasionally.

KitchenAid

Beef **Pot Pie**

● ● ●

½ cup all-purpose flour

1 teaspoon salt, divided

½ teaspoon freshly ground black pepper, divided

1½ pounds beef stew meat

2 tablespoons olive oil

1 pound new red potatoes, cubed

2 cups baby carrots

1 cup frozen pearl onions, thawed

1 parsnip, peeled and cut into 1-inch pieces

1 cup stout, porter or other dark beer

¾ cup beef broth

1 teaspoon chopped fresh thyme *or* ½ teaspoon dried thyme

Perfect Pie Pastry for One-Crust Pie (page 288)

MAKES 4 TO 6 SERVINGS

1 Preheat oven to 350°F. Combine flour, ½ teaspoon salt and ¼ teaspoon pepper in large resealable food storage bag. Add beef and shake to coat.

2 Heat olive oil in large skillet over medium-high heat. Add beef and brown on both sides, turning once. Do not crowd pan. Transfer to 2½- to 3-quart casserole. Add potatoes, carrots, onions and parsnip; mix well.

3 Add stout, broth, thyme, remaining ½ teaspoon salt and ¼ teaspoon pepper to same skillet. Bring to a boil, scraping up browned bits from bottom of skillet. Pour into casserole.

4 Cover; bake 2½ to 3 hours or until meat is fork-tender, stirring once. Let stand, uncovered, at room temperature 15 minutes. Meanwhile, prepare Perfect Pie Pastry for One-Crust Pie.

5 *Increase oven temperature to 425°F.* Place pie pastry over casserole and press edges to seal. Cut slits in crust to vent. Bake 15 to 20 minutes or until crust is golden brown. Cool slightly before serving.

Tuscan Pork Loin Roast with Fig Sauce

• • •

2 tablespoons olive oil

3 cloves garlic, minced

2 teaspoons coarse salt

2 teaspoons dried rosemary

½ teaspoon red pepper flakes or
1 teaspoon black pepper

1 center-cut boneless pork loin roast
(about 3 pounds)

¼ cup dry red wine

1 jar (about 8 ounces)
dried fig spread*

*Dried fig spread can be found with the jams
and jellies in well-stocked supermarkets.

MAKES 6 TO 8 SERVINGS

1 Preheat oven to 350°F. Combine olive oil, garlic, salt, rosemary and red pepper flakes in small bowl; brush over roast. Place roast on rack in shallow roasting pan.

2 Roast 1 hour or until internal temperature of pork reaches 145°F. Transfer to cutting board. Tent with foil; let stand 10 minutes.

3 Pour wine into roasting pan. Cook over medium-high heat, scraping up any browned bits and stirring frequently. Stir in fig spread. Cook until melted and heated through. Slice pork; serve with sauce.

Spicy Citrus Pork with Pineapple Salsa

• • •

1½ teaspoons ground cumin

¼ teaspoon salt

½ teaspoon freshly ground black pepper

1½ pounds center-cut pork loin, rinsed and patted dry

1 tablespoon vegetable oil

2 cans (8 ounces each) pineapple tidbits in juice, drained, ¼ cup juice reserved, divided

2 tablespoons lemon juice, divided

1 teaspoon grated lemon peel

½ cup finely chopped orange or red bell pepper

2 tablespoons finely chopped red onion

1 tablespoon chopped fresh cilantro or mint

½ teaspoon grated fresh ginger (optional)

⅛ teaspoon red pepper flakes (optional)

MAKES 6 SERVINGS

1 Coat 2½-quart slow cooker with nonstick cooking spray. Combine cumin, salt and black pepper in small bowl. Rub all over pork. Heat oil in medium skillet over medium-high heat. Sear pork 1 to 2 minutes per side. Transfer to slow cooker.

2 Spoon 2 tablespoons reserved pineapple juice and 1 tablespoon lemon juice over pork. Cover; cook on LOW 2 to 2¼ hours or on HIGH 1 hour and 10 minutes or until meat thermometer registers 145°F and pork is barely pink in center. Do not overcook.

3 Meanwhile, combine pineapple, remaining 2 tablespoons pineapple juice, remaining 1 tablespoon lemon juice, lemon peel, bell pepper, onion, cilantro, ginger and pepper flakes, if desired, in medium bowl. Toss gently to blend.

4 Transfer pork to serving platter. Let stand 10 minutes before slicing. Slice pork; serve with sauce.

Thai-Style Pork Chops
with Cucumber Sauce

• • •

3 tablespoons Thai peanut sauce*, divided

¼ teaspoon red pepper flakes

4 bone-in pork chops (about 5 ounces each)

1 container (6 ounces) plain yogurt

¼ cup diced unpeeled cucumber

2 tablespoons chopped red onion

2 tablespoons finely chopped fresh mint or cilantro

1 teaspoon sugar

*Thai peanut sauce is located in the Asian section of well-stocked supermarkets.

MAKES 4 SERVINGS

1 Preheat broiler or prepare grill for direct cooking.

2 Combine 2 tablespoons peanut sauce and red pepper flakes in small bowl; brush mixture evenly over both sides of pork. Pork can be refrigerated up to 4 hours at this point.

3 Combine yogurt, cucumber, red onion, mint and sugar in medium bowl; mix well.

4 Broil pork 4 inches from heat source or grill, covered, over medium coals 4 minutes; turn and cook 3 minutes more or until barely pink in center. Baste with remaining 1 tablespoon peanut sauce during last minute of cooking. Serve pork with cucumber sauce.

Tonkatsu (Breaded Pork Cutlets)

• • •

Tonkatsu Sauce (recipe follows)

1 pound pork tenderloin, trimmed

½ cup all-purpose flour

2 eggs

2 tablespoons water

1½ cups panko bread crumbs

6 to 8 tablespoons vegetable oil, divided

Hot cooked rice

MAKES 4 SERVINGS

1 Prepare Tonkatsu Sauce. Set aside.

2 Slice pork diagonally into ½-inch-thick pieces. Place flour in shallow bowl. Whisk eggs and water in another shallow bowl. Place panko in third shallow bowl. Coat pork with flour, then with egg mixture. Roll in panko to coat.

3 Heat 2 tablespoons oil in large nonstick skillet over medium heat. Add pork in single layer; do not crowd pan. Cook 4 minutes on side or until cooked through. Drain on paper towels; keep warm. Repeat with remaining pork, adding additional oil as needed.

4 Serve pork over rice with Tonkatsu Sauce.

Tonkatsu Sauce

¼   **cup ketchup**

1   **tablespoon soy sauce**

2   **teaspoons sugar**

2   **teaspoons mirin (Japanese sweet rice wine)**

1   **teaspoon Worcestershire sauce**

½   **teaspoon grated fresh ginger**

1   **clove garlic, minced**

Combine ketchup, soy sauce, sugar, mirin, Worcestershire, ginger and garlic in small bowl.

Pork with **Spicy Orange Cranberry Sauce**

• • •

1 cup whole-berry cranberry sauce

½ teaspoon grated orange peel

¼ teaspoon ground cinnamon

⅛ teaspoon red pepper flakes

1 teaspoon chili powder

½ teaspoon ground cumin

¼ teaspoon ground allspice

¼ teaspoon salt

¼ teaspoon freshly ground black pepper

4 boneless pork chops (about 1 pound)

1 tablespoon canola oil

MAKES 4 SERVINGS

1 Combine cranberry sauce, orange peel, cinnamon and pepper flakes in small bowl. Set aside.

2 Combine chili powder, cumin, allspice, salt and black pepper in small bowl. Mix well. Sprinkle evenly over both sides of pork.

3 Heat oil in large nonstick skillet over medium heat. Add pork; cook 4 to 5 minutes on each side or until barely pink in center. Serve with cranberry sauce.

Pulled Pork Sandwiches

• • •

2 tablespoons kosher salt

2 tablespoons packed brown sugar

2 tablespoons paprika

1 teaspoon dry mustard

1 teaspoon freshly ground black pepper

1 boneless pork shoulder roast (about 3 pounds)

1½ cups stout, porter or other dark beer

½ cup cider vinegar

6 to 8 Kaiser rolls

¾ cup barbecue sauce

MAKES 6 TO 8 SERVINGS

1 Preheat oven to 325°F. Combine salt, brown sugar, paprika, dry mustard and pepper in small bowl; mix well. Rub all over pork.

2 Place pork in 4-quart Dutch oven. Add beer and vinegar. Cover; bake 3 hours or until meat is fork-tender. Cool 15 to 30 minutes or until cool enough to handle.

3 Shred pork with two forks. Serve warm on rolls with barbecue sauce.

Pork and Corn Bread Stuffing Casserole

• • •

½ teaspoon paprika

¼ teaspoon salt

¼ teaspoon garlic powder

¼ teaspoon freshly ground black pepper

4 bone-in pork chops (about 1¾ pounds)

2 tablespoons butter

1½ cups chopped onions

¾ cup thinly sliced celery

¾ cup matchstick-size carrots

¼ cup chopped fresh parsley

1 can (about 14 ounces) chicken broth

4 cups corn bread stuffing mix

MAKES 4 SERVINGS

1 Preheat oven to 350°F. Spray 13×9-inch baking dish with nonstick cooking spray.

2 Combine paprika, salt, garlic powder and pepper in small bowl. Season both sides of pork chops with paprika mixture.

3 Melt butter in large skillet over medium-high heat. Add pork chops; cook 2 minutes or just until browned. Turn; cook 1 minute. Transfer to plate.

4 Add onions, celery, carrots and parsley to skillet; sauté 4 minutes or until onions are translucent. Add broth; bring to a boil over high heat. Remove from heat; add stuffing and fluff with fork.

5 Transfer mixture to prepared baking dish. Place pork chops on top. Cover; bake 25 minutes or until pork is no longer pink in center.

VARIATION: For a one-skillet meal, use an ovenproof skillet. Place browned pork chops on mixture in skillet; cover and bake as directed.

KitchenAid

Mexican **Pork Sandwiches**

● ● ●

4 cloves garlic, minced

1 teaspoon freshly ground black pepper

Juice of 1 lime

1 tablespoon olive oil

2 onions, thinly sliced

2 jalapeño peppers, seeded and thinly sliced

1 pork tenderloin (about 2 pounds)

8 French dinner rolls

½ to 1 cup tomatillo salsa (salsa verde)

½ cup (2 ounces) shredded Monterey Jack cheese

½ cup chopped fresh cilantro

MAKES 8 SERVINGS

1 Preheat oven to 375°F. Line baking sheet with foil.

2 Combine garlic, black pepper, lime juice and olive oil in small bowl. Spread onions and jalapeños on prepared baking sheet; top with tenderloin. Rub garlic mixture all over tenderloin.

3 Bake 45 minutes or until pork is no longer pink in center (145°F). Wrap ends of foil over pork to keep warm.

4 Split rolls; place cut sides up on ungreased baking sheet. Bake 3 to 5 minutes or until warm.

5 Thinly slice tenderloin. Serve pork on rolls topped with onions, jalapeños, salsa, cheese and cilantro.

Italian Sausage

• • •

3 pounds pork shoulder, cut into 1-inch cubes*

3 teaspoons salt

1½ teaspoons freshly ground black pepper

1¼ teaspoons ground red pepper

2 cloves garlic, minced

1 teaspoon onion powder

1 teaspoon paprika

⅛ teaspoon dried marjoram

⅛ teaspoon dried rosemary

⅛ teaspoon dried thyme

½ cup dry red wine

1 tablespoon shortening

Natural or synthetic casings, prepared for use per package instructions

*Or substitute ground pork from the butcher or supermarket. Stir in spice mixture and wine; proceed with step 5.

MAKES 3 POUNDS SAUSAGE

1 Spread pork on baking sheet; freeze 20 minutes.

2 Combine salt, black pepper, red pepper, garlic, onion powder, paprika, marjoram, rosemary and thyme in small bowl. Sprinkle mixture over pork and toss to coat evenly.

3 Assemble Food Grinder with coarse grinding plate; attach to stand mixer. Grind pork into mixer bowl. Or process meat mixture in batches in food processor until coarsely ground. Transfer batches to the freezer to keep cold.

4 Remove ground pork from freezer. Pour wine over ground pork. Stir vigorously with wooden spoon until well combined.

5 Attach Sausage Stuffer to Food Grinder; grease nozzle with shortening. Slide prepared casings tightly onto nozzle. Tie off end of casing with butcher's twine. Stuff casings according to user guide. Twist sausage into smaller links as desired and refrigerate or freeze until ready to use.

6 Grill, broil or pan-fry sausages until cooked through. Serve hot.

Mozzarella-Pepper Sausage Skillet

● ● ●

1 pound Italian Sausage (page 154)*, casings removed

1 tablespoon olive oil

1 package (8 ounces) sliced mushrooms

1 medium zucchini, thinly sliced

¾ cup finely chopped onion

1 tablespoon dried basil

1 can (8 ounces) tomato sauce

½ cup plain dry bread crumbs

¼ teaspoon salt

1 medium red bell pepper, cut into strips

1 medium green bell pepper, cut into strips

1½ cups (6 ounces) shredded mozzarella cheese

Or use store-bought Italian sausage and remove the casings.

MAKES 4 SERVINGS

1 Prepare Italian Sausage.

2 Heat large nonstick skillet over medium-high heat. Brown sausage, stirring to break up meat. Remove sausage with slotted spoon; drain on paper towels.

3 Add olive oil to skillet. Add mushrooms, zucchini, onion and basil; sauté 5 minutes or until zucchini is soft.

4 Return sausage to skillet. Add tomato sauce, bread crumbs and salt; mix well. Top mixture with bell pepper strips. Simmer, covered, 25 minutes or until peppers are tender. Remove from heat. Top with cheese. Cover; let stand until cheese is melted.

Carribean Pork Chops with Glazed Bell Peppers

• • •

1 cups uncooked brown rice

2 cups water

2 teaspoons Caribbean jerk seasoning, divided

4 bone-in center-cut pork chops, ½-inch thick (about 6 ounces each), trimmed

1 tablespoon olive oil

1 red bell pepper, cut into 1-inch strips

1 yellow bell pepper, cut into 1-inch strips

1 tablespoon balsamic vinegar

1 tablespoon honey

2 teaspoons chopped fresh thyme or parsley

MAKES 4 SERVINGS

1 Combine water and rice in small saucepan; bring to a boil over medium high heat. Reduce heat to low; cover and simmer 40 minutes or until rice is tender. Remove from heat; let stand, covered, 10 minutes. Fluff with fork; set aside.

2 Preheat oven to 375°F. Sprinkle 1 teaspoon jerk seasoning over pork chops. Heat oil in large nonstick skillet over medium-high heat. Add pork chops; cook 2 minutes per side or until browned.

3 Transfer chops to shallow roasting pan or jelly-roll pan. Bake 6 to 8 minutes or just until no longer pink in center.

4 Meanwhile, add bell peppers to same skillet; cook and stir over medium-high heat 3 minutes. Reduce heat to medium. Add vinegar and honey; cook and stir 1 minute. Add rice and remaining 1 teaspoon jerk seasoning. Cook and stir 2 minutes or until heated through.

5 Spoon rice mixture evenly onto four serving plates. Top with pork chops and sprinkle with thyme. Drizzle any juices from roasting pan over chops.

KitchenAid

poultry

Smoked Turkey Breast with Chipotle Rub

• • •

Mesquite or hickory wood chips

2 tablespoons packed dark brown sugar

2 tablespoons ground cumin

1 tablespoon garlic powder

1 tablespoon smoked paprika

1 tablespoon salt

2 teaspoons ground chipotle pepper

1 teaspoon chili powder

¼ cup (½ stick) butter, softened

1 bone-in skin-on turkey breast (5½ to 6 pounds)

MAKES 8 TO 10 SERVINGS

1 Soak wood chips in water at least 30 minutes. Prepare grill for indirect cooking (325° to 350°F).

2 Combine brown sugar, cumin, garlic powder, paprika, salt, ground chipotle and chili powder in small bowl; mix well. Place 2 tablespoons spice mixture in separate small bowl; add butter and mix well.

3 Gently loosen skin over turkey breast; spread butter mixture under skin. Rub skin and cavity of turkey with remaining dry spice mixture.

4 Place some of wood chips in small disposable aluminum pan. Place tray under grid directly on heat source; let wood to begin to smolder, about 10 minutes. Place turkey on grid away from heat source.

5 Grill, covered, 1 hour. Add additional wood chips. Grill 1 to 1½ hours or until thermometer inserted into thickest part of turkey not touching bone registers 170°F. Transfer to cutting board; let stand 10 minutes before slicing.

KitchenAid

Drunken **Roast Chicken**

• • •

1 whole chicken, quartered
(3 to 3½ pounds)

¼ cup soy sauce

¼ cup dry sherry, divided

4 cloves garlic, minced

1 tablespoon minced fresh ginger

½ teaspoon red pepper flakes

½ cup plum sauce

2 teaspoons Chinese hot mustard

MAKES 4 SERVINGS

1 Place chicken in large resealable food storage bag. Combine soy sauce, 3 tablespoons sherry, garlic, ginger and red pepper flakes in small bowl; pour over chicken. Seal bag; turn to coat. Marinate in refrigerator at least 30 minutes or up to 4 hours.

2 Meanwhile, combine plum sauce, mustard and remaining 1 tablespoon sherry in small bowl; mix well. Set aside.

3 Preheat oven to 375°F. Line large baking sheet or jelly-roll pan with foil. Remove chicken from bag, reserving marinade. Place chicken on prepared baking sheet.

4 Bake 25 minutes. Brush reserved marinade over chicken; discard any remaining marinade. *Increase oven temperature to 450°F.* Bake 20 minutes or until thermometer inserted into thigh registers 165°F. Serve chicken with plum sauce mixture.

Italian Country-Style **Braised Chicken**

● ● ●

¾ cup boiling water

½ cup dried porcini mushrooms (about ½ ounce)

¼ cup all-purpose flour

1 teaspoon salt

½ teaspoon freshly ground black pepper

1 whole chicken, cut up (3½ to 4 pounds)

3 tablespoons olive oil

2 ounces pancetta or bacon, chopped

1 medium onion, chopped

2 carrots, thinly sliced

3 cloves garlic, minced

1 cup chicken broth

1 tablespoon tomato paste

1 cup green Italian olives

MAKES 4 TO 6 SERVINGS

1 Pour boiling water over mushrooms in small bowl. Let stand 15 to 20 minutes or until mushrooms are tender.

2 Meanwhile, combine flour, salt and pepper in large resealable food storage bag. Add one or two pieces of chicken at a time; toss to coat. Discard any remaining flour mixture.

3 Heat oil in large skillet over medium heat. Brown chicken on both sides about 15 minutes or until golden brown. Transfer chicken to plate; set aside.

4 Pour off all but 1 tablespoon oil from skillet. Add pancetta, onion and carrots; cook 5 minutes, stirring occasionally to scrape up browned bits. Add garlic; cook 1 minute. Strain mushrooms, reserving liquid. Chop mushrooms. Add mushrooms and reserved liquid to skillet. Add broth and tomato paste; bring to a boil over high heat.

5 Return chicken and any accumulated juices to skillet. Reduce heat; simmer, uncovered, 20 minutes or until chicken is cooked through and sauce thickens, turning once. Stir in olives; heat through. Transfer chicken to serving platter; top with sauce.

Oven Barbecued Chicken

• • •

2 tablespoons vegetable oil, divided

1 large onion, chopped

⅓ cup packed dark brown sugar

⅓ cup cider vinegar

1 can (28 ounces) tomato purée

2 teaspoons chili powder

1 teaspoon ground mustard

1¼ teaspoons salt, divided

1 teaspoon freshly ground black pepper, divided

¼ teaspoon liquid smoke

1 whole chicken, cut into 8 pieces (6 to 7 pounds)

MAKES 8 TO 10 SERVINGS

1 Heat 1 tablespoon oil in medium saucepan over medium-high heat. Add onion; sauté about 5 minutes or until softened. Stir in brown sugar and vinegar. Add tomato purée, chili powder, mustard, 1 teaspoon salt, ¾ teaspoon pepper and liquid smoke, stirring until well blended. Bring to a boil. Reduce heat; simmer 45 minutes until mixture thickens slightly, stirring occasionally.

2 Meanwhile, preheat oven to 450°F. Place chicken on baking sheet. Brush with remaining 1 tablespoon oil and season with remaining ¼ teaspoon salt and ¼ teaspoon pepper.

3 Roast chicken 35 minutes or until almost cooked through (internal temperature of thigh registers 160°F). Preheat broiler. Spread sauce all over chicken. Broil 6 inches from heat source 10 minutes or until chicken is cooked through (165°F) and begins to brown.

KitchenAid

Chicken **Piccata**

● ● ●

3 tablespoons all-purpose flour

½ teaspoon salt

¼ teaspoon freshly ground black pepper

4 boneless skinless chicken breasts (4 ounces each)

2 teaspoons olive oil

1 teaspoon butter

2 cloves garlic, minced

¾ cup chicken broth

1 tablespoon fresh lemon juice

2 tablespoons chopped fresh Italian parsley

1 tablespoon drained capers

MAKES 4 SERVINGS

1 Combine flour, salt and pepper in shallow bowl. Reserve 1 tablespoon flour mixture.

2 Place chicken between sheets of plastic wrap. Pound chicken to ½-inch thickness with flat side of meat mallet or rolling pin. Coat chicken with flour mixture, shaking off excess.

3 Heat oil and butter in large nonstick skillet over medium heat until butter is melted. Cook chicken 4 to 5 minutes on each side or until no longer pink in center. Transfer to serving platter; cover loosely with foil.

4 Add garlic to same skillet; sauté over medium heat 1 minute. Add reserved flour mixture; cook and stir 1 minute. Add broth and lemon juice; cook, stirring frequently, 2 minutes or until sauce thickens. Stir in parsley and capers; spoon sauce over chicken.

Beer-Brined Chicken

• • •

4 cups water

3 cups stout, porter or other dark beer

2 cups apple juice

½ cup plus ½ teaspoon kosher salt, divided

½ cup packed brown sugar

1 teaspoon paprika

1 sprig fresh rosemary

1 bay leaf

1 whole chicken (3½ to 4 pounds)

¼ cup (½ stick) butter, melted

1 tablespoon chopped fresh rosemary

¼ teaspoon freshly ground black pepper

MAKES 2 TO 4 SERVINGS

1 Combine water, beer, apple juice, ½ cup salt, brown sugar, paprika, rosemary sprig and bay leaf in Dutch oven. Stir until salt and sugar are dissolved. Add chicken; cover and refrigerate 2 to 4 hours.

2 Preheat oven to 425°F. Remove chicken from brine; pat dry. Tie drumsticks together to maintain best shape. Place on rack in roasting pan. Cover loosely with foil; roast 45 minutes. Meanwhile, combine butter, chopped rosemary, remaining ½ teaspoon salt and pepper in small bowl.

3 Remove foil. Brush butter mixture all over chicken. Roast 30 to 45 minutes or until thermometer inserted into thigh registers 165°F. Cover loosely with foil if chicken begins to get too dark.

4 Let stand 10 minutes before carving.

KitchenAid

Mediterranean **Chicken Kabobs**

• • •

2 pounds boneless skinless chicken breasts or chicken tenders, cut into 1-inch pieces

1 small eggplant, peeled and cut into 1-inch pieces

1 medium zucchini, cut crosswise into ½-inch slices

2 medium onions, each cut into 8 wedges

16 medium mushrooms, stems removed

16 cherry tomatoes

1 cup chicken broth

⅔ cup balsamic vinegar

3 tablespoons olive oil

2 tablespoons dried mint

4 teaspoons dried basil

1 tablespoon dried oregano

Cooked couscous (optional)

MAKES 8 SERVINGS

1 Thread chicken, eggplant, zucchini, onions, mushrooms and tomatoes alternately onto 16 metal skewers; place in large glass baking dish.

2 Combine broth, vinegar, oil, mint, basil and oregano in small bowl; pour over kabobs. Cover and marinate in refrigerator 2 hours, turning occasionally. Remove kabobs from marinade; discard marinade.

3 Preheat broiler. Broil kabobs 6 inches from heat 10 to 15 minutes or until chicken is cooked through, turning kabobs halfway through cooking time. Serve over couscous, if desired.

Lemony **Greek Chicken**

• • •

1 whole chicken, cut up
(about 3 to 4 pounds)

1 tablespoon olive oil

2 teaspoons Greek seasoning

1 teaspoon salt

1 teaspoon freshly ground black pepper

Juice of 1 lemon

MAKES 4 TO 6 SERVINGS

1 Preheat oven to 400°F.

2 Brush chicken with oil. Arrange bone side down in two large baking dishes. Combine Greek seasoning, salt and pepper in small bowl; sprinkle half of mixture over chicken. Bake 30 minutes.

3 Turn chicken pieces over. Sprinkle with remaining seasoning mixture and lemon juice. Bake 30 minutes or until chicken is cooked through (165°F).

Cornish Hens with Wild Rice Stuffing

• • •

2 tablespoons butter

2 stalks celery, cut into
½-inch pieces

¾ cup dried apricots

2 cups cooked wild and white rice

½ teaspoon salt

⅛ teaspoon allspice

4 Cornish hens
(1½ pounds each)

8 slices bacon

MAKES 4 SERVINGS

1 Preheat oven to 350°F.

2 Melt butter in medium skillet over medium heat. Add celery; sauté 2 minutes. Transfer celery to food processor. Add apricots; process until finely chopped. PLace mixture in large bowl. Add butter from skillet, rice, salt and allspice; mix well.

3 Stuff hens with rice mixture. Tie drumsticks together and crisscross two strips of bacon over each hen. Place on rack in baking pan. Bake 1½ to 2 hours or until thermometer inserted into thigh registers 165°F. Serve immediately.

KitchenAid

Glazed **Cornish Hens**

• • •

2 Cornish hens (1½ pounds each)

3 tablespoons fresh lemon juice

1 clove garlic, minced

¼ cup orange marmalade

1 tablespoon coarse grain mustard

2 teaspoons grated fresh ginger

MAKES 4 SERVINGS

1 Remove giblets from cavities of hens; reserve for another use or discard. Split hens in half on cutting board with sharp knife or poultry shears, cutting through breastbones and backbones. Rinse hens with cold water; pat dry with paper towels. Place hens in large resealable food storage bag.

2 Combine lemon juice and garlic in small bowl; pour over hens. Seal bag; turn to coat. Marinate in refrigerator 30 minutes.

3 Meanwhile, prepare grill for direct cooking.

4 Drain hens, discarding marinade. Place hens, skin side up, on grid. Grill hens, covered, over medium heat 20 minutes.

5 Meanwhile, combine marmalade, mustard and ginger in small bowl. Brush half of marmalade mixture evenly over hens. Grill, covered, 10 minutes. Brush with remaining mixture. Grill, covered, 5 to 10 minutes or until thermometer inserted into thigh registers 165°F. Serve immediately.

KitchenAid

Chicken **Cassoulet**

● ● ●

4 slices bacon

¼ cup all-purpose flour

Salt and freshly ground black pepper

1¾ pounds bone-in chicken pieces

2 chicken sausages (2¼ ounces each), cooked and cut into ¼-inch pieces

1 medium onion, chopped

1½ cups diced red and green bell peppers (about 2 small bell peppers)

2 cloves garlic, finely chopped

1 teaspoon dried thyme

1 teaspoon olive oil

2 cans (about 15 ounces each) cannellini or Great Northern beans, rinsed and drained

½ cup dry white wine

MAKES 6 SERVINGS

1 Preheat oven to 350°F. Cook bacon in large skillet over medium-high heat until crisp; drain on paper towels. Cut into 1-inch pieces.

2 Pour off all but 2 tablespoons fat from skillet. Place flour in shallow bowl; season with salt and black pepper. Coat chicken pieces with flour mixture; shake off excess. Brown chicken in batches in skillet over medium-high heat; remove and set aside. Lightly brown sausages in same skillet; remove and set aside.

3 Add onion, bell peppers, garlic and thyme to skillet; season with salt and black pepper. Sauté over medium heat 5 minutes or until softened, adding olive oil as needed to prevent sticking. Transfer onion mixture to 13×9-inch baking dish. Add beans; mix well. Top with chicken, sausages and bacon. Add wine to skillet; cook over medium heat, scraping up browned bits from bottom of skillet. Pour over casserole.

4 Cover; bake 40 minutes. Uncover; bake 15 minutes or until chicken is cooked through (165°F).

fish and seafood

Lobster Tails with Tasty Butters

• • •

Hot and Spicy Butter,
Scallion Butter
or Chili-Mustard Butter
(recipes follow)

4 fresh or thawed frozen lobster tails
(about 5 ounces each)

MAKES 4 SERVINGS

1 Prepare grill for direct cooking. Prepare desired butters.

2 Rinse lobster tails in cold water. Butterfly tails by cutting lengthwise through centers of hard top shells and meat. Cut to, but not through, bottoms of shells. Press shell halves of tails apart with fingers. Brush lobster meat with butter mixture.

3 Place tails on grid, meat side down. Grill, uncovered, over medium-high heat 4 minutes. Turn tails, meat side up. Brush with butter mixture; grill 4 to 5 minutes or until lobster meat turns opaque.

4 Heat remaining butter mixture, stirring occasionally. Serve butter mixture for dipping.

Hot and Spicy Butter

⅓ **cup butter, melted**

1 **tablespoon finely chopped onion**

2 **to 3 teaspoons hot pepper sauce**

1 **teaspoon dried thyme**

¼ **teaspoon ground allspice**

Scallion Butter

⅓ **cup butter, melted**

1 **tablespoon finely chopped green onion**

1 **tablespoon fresh lemon juice**

1 **tablespoon freshly grated lemon peel**

¼ **teaspoon freshly ground black pepper**

Chili-Mustard Butter

⅓ **cup butter, melted**

1 **tablespoon finely chopped onion**

1 **tablespoon Dijon mustard**

1 **teaspoon chili powder**

For each butter sauce, combine ingredients in small bowl.

KitchenAid

Crisp Lemony **Baked Fish**

• • •

1¼ cups crushed corn flakes

¼ cup shredded Parmesan cheese

2 tablespoons minced green onions

⅛ teaspoon freshly ground black pepper

1 lemon

1 egg

4 small haddock fillets
(3 to 4 ounces each)

MAKES 4 SERVINGS

1 Preheat oven to 400°F. Line baking sheet with parchment paper.

2 Combine corn flakes, cheese, green onions and pepper in shallow bowl. Grate lemon peel; stir into corn flake mixture. Reserve lemon. Whisk egg in another shallow bowl.

3 Coat fish with egg, then with corn flake mixture. Place on prepared baking sheet.

4 Bake about 10 minutes or until cooked through. Cut reserved lemon into wedges; serve fish with lemon wedges.

KitchenAid

Prosciutto-Wrapped **Snapper**

• • •

1 tablespoon plus 1 teaspoon
olive oil, divided

2 cloves garlic, minced

4 skinless red snapper fillets or halibut
(about 6 to 7 ounces each)

½ teaspoon salt

½ teaspoon freshly ground black pepper

8 large fresh sage leaves

8 thin slices prosciutto (4 ounces)

¼ cup dry Marsala wine

MAKES 4 SERVINGS

1 Preheat oven to 400°F.

2 Combine 1 tablespoon oil and garlic in small bowl; brush over fish. Sprinkle with salt and pepper. Lay two sage leaves on each fillet. Wrap two prosciutto slices around fish to enclose sage leaves and most of the fish. Tuck in ends of prosciutto.

3 Heat remaining 1 teaspoon oil in large ovenproof skillet over medium-high heat. Add fish, top sides down; cook 3 to 4 minutes or until prosciutto is crisp. Carefully turn fish. Transfer skillet to oven; bake 8 to 10 minutes or until fish is opaque in center.

4 Transfer fish to serving plates; keep warm. Pour wine into skillet. Cook over medium-high heat, scraping up browned bits. Stir constantly 2 to 3 minutes or until mixture has reduced by half. Drizzle over fish.

Cedar Plank Salmon
with Grilled Citrus Mango

• • •

4 salmon fillets (6 ounces each), skin intact

2 teaspoons sugar, divided

1 teaspoon chili powder

½ teaspoon freshly ground black pepper

¼ teaspoon salt

¼ teaspoon ground allspice

1 tablespoon fresh lemon juice

1 tablespoon fresh lime juice

2 tablespoons fresh orange juice

2 teaspoons minced fresh ginger

¼ cup chopped fresh mint

⅛ teaspoon red pepper flakes

2 medium mangoes, peeled and cut into 1-inch pieces

1 cedar plank (about 15 × 7 inches, ½-inch thick), soaked*

*Soak in water 5 hours or overnight.

MAKES 4 SERVINGS

1 Oil grid. Prepare grill for direct cooking.

2 Rinse and pat dry salmon fillets. Combine 1 teaspoon sugar, chili powder, black pepper, salt and allspice in small bowl. Rub evenly over flesh side of fillets. Set aside.

3 Combine remaining 1 teaspoon sugar, lemon juice, lime juice, orange juice, ginger, mint and red pepper flakes in medium bowl. Set aside.

4 Thread mango pieces onto skewers or spread out in grill basket.

5 Place soaked plank on grid; grill, covered, over medium heat until plank smokes and crackles.* Place salmon, skin side down, on plank and place mango skewers on grid. Grill, covered, 6 to 8 minutes, until mango is slightly charred, turning skewers frequently. Remove mango; set aside. Grill salmon, covered, 9 to 12 minutes without turning until fish begins to flake when tested with fork.

6 Remove plank from grill and transfer salmon to serving platter. Slide mango pieces off skewers and add to mint mixture; toss gently to coat. Serve immediately with salmon.

NOTE: If you do not have a cedar plank, the salmon may be cooked directly on the grill. Follow steps 1 through 5; lightly brush grid with oil; and place salmon on grid. Grill 6 to 8 minutes per side or until fish flakes easily with a fork.

*If plank begins to burn or flare up, spray with water from a clean spray bottle.

○ **TIP**

CEDAR PLANKS CAN BE PURCHASED AT GOURMET KITCHEN STORES OR HARDWARE STORES. BE SURE TO BUY UNTREATED WOOD AT LEAST ½-INCH THICK.

KitchenAid

Spicy **Crabmeat Frittata**

• • •

6 eggs

1 can (6½ ounces) lump white crabmeat, drained and large pieces broken up

¼ teaspoon freshly ground black pepper

¼ teaspoon salt

¼ teaspoon hot pepper sauce

1 tablespoon olive oil

1 medium green bell pepper, finely chopped

2 cloves garlic, minced

1 large ripe plum tomato, seeded and finely chopped

MAKES 4 SERVINGS

1 Preheat broiler. beat eggs in medium bowl. Add crabmeat, black pepper, salt and hot pepper sauce to eggs; blend well. Set aside.

2 Heat oil in medium ovenproof nonstick skillet over medium-high heat. Add bell pepper and garlic; sauté 3 minutes or until soft.

3 Add tomato; sauté 1 minute. Add egg mixture. Reduce heat to medium-low; cook about 7 minutes or until eggs begin to set around edges.

4 Broil 6 inches from heat source about 2 minutes or until frittata is set and top is browned. Remove from broiler; slide frittata onto serving plate. Serve immediately.

Rosemary-Garlic Scallops with Polenta

• • •

2 teaspoons olive oil

1 medium red bell pepper, sliced

⅓ cup chopped red onion

3 cloves garlic, minced

½ pound fresh bay scallops

2 teaspoons chopped fresh rosemary or
¾ teaspoon dried rosemary

¼ teaspoon freshly ground black pepper

1¼ cups chicken broth

½ cup cornmeal

¼ teaspoon salt

MAKES 2 SERVINGS

1 Heat oil in large nonstick skillet over medium heat. Add bell pepper, onion and garlic; sauté 5 minutes. Add scallops, rosemary and black pepper. Cook 3 to 5 minutes or until scallops are opaque, stirring occasionally.

2 Meanwhile, combine broth, cornmeal and salt in small saucepan. Bring to a boil over high heat. Reduce heat to low; simmer 5 minutes or until polenta is very thick, stirring frequently. Transfer to serving plates. Top polenta with scallop mixture.

Stir-Fried Crab

• • •

8 ounces firm tofu, drained

1 tablespoon soy sauce

¼ cup chicken broth

3 tablespoons oyster sauce

2 teaspoons cornstarch

Sesame Noodle Cake
(recipe follows)

1 tablespoon peanut
or vegetable oil

6 ounces (2 cups) fresh snow peas, cut
into halves

8 ounces thawed frozen cooked
crabmeat or imitation crabmeat, broken
into ½-inch pieces
(about 2 cups)

2 tablespoons chopped
fresh cilantro or thinly sliced
green onions

MAKES 4 SERVINGS

1 Press tofu lightly between paper towels; cut into ½-inch squares or triangles. Place in shallow dish. Drizzle soy sauce over tofu.

2 Blend broth and oyster sauce into cornstarch in small bowl until smooth.

3 Prepare Sesame Noodle Cake.

4 Heat wok or large skillet over medium-high heat. Add oil; heat until hot. Add snow peas; stir-fry 3 minutes. Add crabmeat; stir-fry 1 minute. Stir broth mixture and add to wok. Stir-fry 30 seconds or until sauce boils and thickens.

5 Stir in tofu; heat through. Serve over Sesame Noodle Cake; sprinkle with cilantro.

Sesame Noodle Cake

4   ounces uncooked Chinese egg noodles

1   tablespoon soy sauce

1   tablespoon peanut or vegetable oil

½   teaspoon dark sesame oil

1 Cook noodles according to package directions; drain well. Place in large bowl. Toss with soy sauce.

2 Heat peanut oil in medium nonstick skillet over medium heat. Add noodle mixture; pat into even layer with spatula.

3 Cook 6 minutes or until bottom is lightly browned. Invert onto plate, then slide back into skillet, browned side up. Cook 4 minutes or until bottom is browned. Drizzle with sesame oil. Transfer to serving platter and cut into quarters.

Tuna Sicilian Style

• • •

¾ cup extra virgin olive oil

Juice of 2 lemons

4 cloves garlic, minced

1 tablespoon chopped fresh rosemary *or*
1½ teaspoons dried rosemary

1 tablespoon chopped fresh parsley

¾ teaspoon salt

½ teaspoon freshly ground black pepper

4 fresh tuna steaks, ½ inch thick

Lemon slices (optional)

Arugula or spinach (optional)

MAKES 4 SERVINGS

1 Prepare grill for direct cooking. Combine olive oil, lemon juice, garlic, rosemary, parsley, salt and pepper in small bowl; reserve half of mixture for serving.

2 Brush both sides of tuna with remaining olive oil mixture. Grill* tuna over medium-high heat 8 minutes or until desired degree of doneness, turning once and brushing frequently with sauce. Add lemon slices to grill during last minute of cooking, if desired.

3 Meanwhile, heat reserved sauce in small saucepan over low heat. Serve with tuna and arugula, if desired. Garnish with lemon slices.

Or cook in grill pan on stovetop.

KitchenAid

Cherry-Stuffed **Perch Rolls**

● ● ●

2 tablespoons butter, divided

¼ cup onion, finely chopped

¼ cup celery, finely chopped

1 cup diced sourdough or Italian bread

½ cup dried cherries, chopped

¼ cup shelled salted pistachio nuts, coarsely chopped

¼ teaspoon salt, divided

¼ teaspoon freshly ground black pepper, divided

4 perch fillets (about 6 ounces each)

MAKES 4 SERVINGS

1 Preheat oven to 400°F. Spray 9-inch glass pie plate with nonstick cooking spray. Melt 1 tablespoon butter in medium skillet over medium-high heat. Add onion and celery; sauté 3 minutes. Add bread cubes, dried cherries, pistachios, ⅛ teaspoon salt and ⅛ teaspoon pepper; cook 1 minute, stirring constantly. Remove from heat; let cool slightly.

2 Shape perch fillets into rolls; stand up in prepared pie plate and secure with toothpicks. Spoon ¼ cup cherry filling into center of each perch roll. Melt remaining 1 tablespoon butter; drizzle over perch. Sprinkle with remaining ⅛ teaspoon salt and ⅛ teaspoon pepper. Cover loosely with foil.

3 Bake 10 minutes. Remove foil; bake 5 minutes or until perch is opaque and filling is lightly browned.

Orange-Glazed **Salmon**

• • •

2 tablespoons orange juice

2 tablespoons soy sauce

1 tablespoon honey

¾ teaspoon grated fresh ginger

½ teaspoon rice wine vinegar

¼ teaspoon sesame oil

4 salmon fillets
(about 6 ounces each)

½ teaspoon salt

¼ teaspoon freshly ground black pepper

1 tablespoon olive oil

MAKES 4 SERVINGS

1 For glaze, whisk orange juice, soy sauce, honey, ginger, vinegar and sesame oil in small bowl.

2 Season salmon with salt and pepper. Heat olive oil in medium nonstick skillet over medium-high heat. Place salmon, skin side up, in skillet; brush with glaze. Cook salmon 4 minutes or just until center is opaque. Carefully turn; brush with some of remaining glaze. Cook 4 minutes or until salmon just begins to flake when tested with fork. Transfer salmon to serving plate; cover and keep warm.

3 Meanwhile, place remaining glaze in small saucepan; cook and stir until thickened and reduced to about 2 tablespoons. Serve over salmon.

KitchenAid

Beer and Chipotle **Fish Tacos**

• • •

1½ pounds cod, grouper or other white fish fillets, cut into thin strips

1 bottle (12 ounces) pale ale or light-colored beer

½ cup yellow cornmeal

1 teaspoon chipotle chili powder

½ teaspoon salt

2 tablespoons olive oil

6 to 8 (6-inch) white corn tortillas, warmed

1½ cups shredded cabbage

Lime juice, chopped fresh tomatoes, chopped fresh cilantro, salsa and sour cream (optional)

MAKES 6 TO 8 SERVINGS

1 Place fish in shallow bowl. Pour beer over fish; marinate 15 to 30 minutes.

2 Combine cornmeal, chipotle chili powder and salt in another shallow bowl. Drain fish; coat with cornmeal mixture.

3 Heat oil in large skillet over medium-high heat. Cook fish about 3 minutes on each side or until golden brown.

4 Serve fish in tortillas with cabbage; drizzle with lime juice and top with tomatoes, cilantro, salsa and sour cream, if desired.

Salmon and **Crab Cakes**

• • •

½ pound cooked salmon

½ pound cooked crabmeat*

1 egg, lightly beaten

1½ tablespoons mayonnaise

1 tablespoon minced fresh parsley

1 teaspoon dried dill weed

½ teaspoon salt

½ teaspoon freshly ground black pepper

½ teaspoon mustard

¼ teaspoon Worcestershire sauce

¼ cup plain dry bread crumbs

Nonstick cooking spray

Lump crabmeat works best.

MAKES 4 SERVINGS

1 Combine salmon and crabmeat in medium bowl; flake with fork. Add egg, mayonnaise, parsley, dill, salt, pepper, mustard and Worcestershire; stir until well blended.

2 Place bread crumbs in shallow bowl. Drop fish mixture by heaping ⅓ cupfuls into bread crumbs; shape into thick patties and coat with crumbs.

3 Spray large nonstick skillet with cooking spray. Cook fish cakes, covered, over medium heat 5 to 8 minutes, turning once.

KitchenAid

Grilled **Swordfish** Sicilian Style

● ● ●

3 tablespoons extra virgin olive oil

1 clove garlic, minced

2 tablespoons fresh lemon juice

¾ teaspoon salt

⅛ teaspoon freshly ground black pepper

3 tablespoons capers, drained

1 tablespoon chopped fresh oregano or basil

1½ pounds swordfish steaks, ¾ inch thick

MAKES 4 TO 6 SERVINGS

1 Oil grid. Prepare grill for direct cooking.

2 For sauce, heat oil in small saucepan over low heat; add garlic. Cook 1 minute. Remove from heat; cool slightly. Whisk in lemon juice, salt and pepper until salt is dissolved. Stir in capers and oregano.

3 Grill swordfish over medium heat 7 to 8 minutes or until centers are opaque, turning once. Serve with sauce.

Lemon Shrimp with Black Beans and Rice

• • •

1 cup uncooked instant brown rice

⅛ teaspoon ground turmeric

½ (15-ounce) can black beans, rinsed and drained

1 medium poblano pepper or ½ green bell pepper, minced

1½ to 2 teaspoons grated lemon peel

3 tablespoons fresh lemon juice

3 tablespoons extra virgin olive oil, divided

⅛ teaspoon salt

1 pound raw shrimp, peeled and deveined (with tails on)

1½ teaspoons chili powder

MAKES 4 SERVINGS

1 Cook rice according to package directions, adding turmeric to water with rice.

2 Combine beans, poblano, lemon peel, lemon juice, 2 tablespoons oil and salt in medium bowl. Set aside.

3 Heat remaining 1 tablespoon oil in large nonstick skillet over medium heat. Add shrimp and chili powder; sauté 4 minutes or until shrimp are pink and opaque. Add bean mixture; sauté 1 minute or until heated through.

4 Serve shrimp mixture with rice.

KitchenAid

Herb- and **Lemon-Scented Tilapia**

● ● ● ●

1 cup minced fresh Italian parsley

½ cup minced fresh chives

¾ teaspoon salt, divided

½ teaspoon freshly ground black pepper, divided

1 lemon

4 large tilapia fillets (about 4 ounces each)

1 tablespoon olive oil

4 tablespoons butter, divided

MAKES 4 SERVINGS

1 Combine parsley, chives, ½ teaspoon salt and ¼ teaspoon pepper in shallow bowl. Grate lemon peel over herbs; toss to combine. Reserve lemon.

2 Brush olive oil over fish; coat with herb mixture.

3 Melt 2 tablespoons butter in large skillet over medium heat. Add tilapia. Cook 3 to 4 minutes on each side or until fish flakes easily when tested with fork. Transfer to serving platter; keep warm.

4 Melt remaining 2 tablespoons butter in same skillet over low heat. Cut lemon in half; squeeze juice from one half into skillet. Stir in remaining ¼ teaspoon salt and ¼ teaspoon pepper. Pour over fish. Slice remaining lemon half for garnish. Serve immediately.

Southern Fried Catfish with Hush Puppies

• • •

Hush Puppy Batter
(recipe follows)

4 catfish fillets (about 6 ounces each)

½ cup yellow cornmeal

3 tablespoons all-purpose flour

1½ teaspoons salt

¼ teaspoon ground red pepper

Vegetable oil

MAKES 4 SERVINGS

1 Prepare Hush Puppy Batter.

2 Rinse catfish; pat dry with paper towels. Combine cornmeal, flour, salt and red pepper in shallow bowl. Coat fish with cornmeal mixture. Heat 1 inch oil in large heavy skillet over medium heat until 375°F on deep-fry thermometer.

3 Cook fish in batches 4 to 5 minutes or until golden brown and fish begins to flake when tested with fork. Allow temperature of oil to return to 375°F between batches. Drain fish on paper towels.

4 Drop Hush Puppy Batter by tablespoonfuls into hot oil. Cook in batches 2 minutes or until golden brown. Drain on paper towels. Serve with fish.

Hush Puppy Batter

1½   cups yellow cornmeal

½   cup all-purpose flour

2   teaspoons baking powder

½   teaspoon salt

1   cup milk

1   small onion, minced

1   egg, lightly beaten

Combine cornmeal, flour, baking powder and salt in medium bowl. Add milk, onion and egg. Stir until well blended. Let stand 5 to 10 minutes before frying.

vegetarian entrées

Vegetable Fajitas with Spicy Salsa

● ● ●

SPICY SALSA

3 whole medium tomatoes

1 small unpeeled onion

1 jalapeño pepper

6 cloves unpeeled garlic

Juice of 1 lime

1 teaspoon salt

VEGETABLE FAJITAS

12 (8-inch) flour tortillas

1 tablespoon canola oil

4 medium bell peppers, cut into strips

1 medium red onion, peeled, cut in half vertically and thickly sliced

1 teaspoon salt

Freshly ground black pepper (optional)

1 can (about 16 ounces) vegetarian refried beans

Chopped fresh cilantro and sour cream (optional)

MAKES 6 SERVINGS

1 For salsa, preheat broiler. Line baking sheet with parchment paper or foil. Place tomatoes, onion, jalapeño and garlic on prepared baking sheet. Broil 10 minutes. Turn vegetables and rotate pan. Broil 10 minutes or until blackened. Cool 10 minutes. Peel tomatoes, onion and garlic; peel and seed jalapeño. Place in blender or food processor with lime juice and salt; process until desired consistency. Refrigerate until ready to serve.

2 For fajitas, heat cast iron or heavy skillet over medium-high heat. Cook tortillas one at a time 15 seconds on each side or until blistered and browned; keep warm.

3 Reduce heat to medium; heat oil in skillet. Add bell pepper strips, red onion slices, salt and black pepper, if desired; cook 10 minutes or until onion is cooked through and peppers are crisp-tender, stirring occasionally.

4 Heat refried beans in small saucepan over medium heat. Spread about 2 tablespoons beans on each tortilla; top with ⅓ cup vegetables and about 2 tablespoons salsa. Roll up; serve immediately with cilantro and sour cream, if desired.

KitchenAid

Fried Tofu with Asian Vegetables

• • •

1 package (about 14 ounces) firm tofu

½ cup soy sauce, divided

1 cup all-purpose flour

¾ teaspoon salt, divided

⅛ teaspoon freshly ground black pepper

Vegetable oil for frying

2 packages (16 ounces each) frozen mixed Asian vegetables*

3 tablespoons water

1 teaspoon cornstarch

3 tablespoons plum sauce

2 tablespoons lemon juice

2 teaspoons sugar

1 teaspoon minced fresh ginger

⅛ to ¼ teaspoon red pepper flakes

Frozen vegetables do not need to be thawed before cooking.

MAKES 6 SERVINGS

1 Drain tofu; cut into ¾-inch cubes. Gently mix tofu and ¼ cup soy sauce in shallow bowl; let stand 5 minutes. Combine flour, ½ teaspoon salt and black pepper on plate. Add tofu to flour mixture in batches; toss to coat.

2 Heat 1½ inches oil in wok or Dutch oven. Test heat by dropping one tofu cube into oil; it should brown in 1 minute. Fry tofu cubes in small batches until browned. Remove from oil with slotted spoon; drain on paper towels.

3 Pour off all but 1 tablespoon oil from wok. Add frozen vegetables and remaining ¼ teaspoon salt. Cook over medium-high heat about 6 minutes, stirring occasionally, or until vegetables are heated through. Increase heat to high to evaporate any remaining liquid. Set aside and cover to keep warm.

4 Stir water into cornstarch in small bowl until smooth. Combine cornstarch mixture, remaining ¼ cup soy sauce, plum sauce, lemon juice, sugar, ginger and red pepper flakes in small saucepan; cook and stir over low heat 1 to 2 minutes or until sauce is slightly thickened.

5 Spoon vegetables into serving bowl. Top with tofu and sauce; toss gently to mix.

KitchenAid

Eggplant Parmigiana

• • •

2 eggs

¼ cup milk

Dash garlic powder

Dash onion powder

Salt and freshly ground black pepper

½ cup seasoned dry bread crumbs

1 large eggplant, cut into ½-inch-thick slices

Vegetable oil for frying

1 jar (about 26 ounces) pasta sauce

4 cups (16 ounces) shredded mozzarella cheese

2½ cups (10 ounces) shredded Swiss cheese

¼ cup grated Parmesan cheese

¼ cup grated Romano cheese

MAKES 4 SERVINGS

1 Preheat oven to 350°F. Whisk eggs, milk, garlic powder, onion powder, salt and pepper in shallow bowl. Place bread crumbs in another shallow bowl. Coat eggplant with egg mixture, then with bread crumbs.

2 Heat ¼ inch oil in large skillet over medium-high heat. Brown eggplant in batches on both sides; drain on paper towels.

3 Spread 3 tablespoons pasta sauce over bottom of 13×9-inch baking dish. Layer half of eggplant, half of mozzarella cheese, half of Swiss cheese and half of remaining sauce in dish. Repeat layers. Sprinkle with Parmesan and Romano cheeses.

4 Bake 30 minutes or until heated through and cheeses are melted.

Vegetarian Sushi Maki

• • •

Sushi Rice (recipe follows)

6 to 8 sheets toasted sushi nori

1 teaspoon wasabi
or prepared mustard

1 ripe avocado, thinly sliced

6 to 8 thin strips peeled cucumber

1 cup spinach leaves,
finely shredded

½ cup thinly sliced steamed carrot

6 to 8 teaspoons toasted
sesame seeds

Pickled ginger

Soy sauce

MAKES 6 TO 8 ROLLS

1 Prepare Sushi Rice.

2 Place one sheet of nori on flat work surface. Cover bottom third of sheet with thin layer of wasabi. Spread about ⅓ cup rice on top of wasabi, leaving 1 inch uncovered along bottom edge. Arrange avocado, cucumber, spinach, carrot and sesame seeds on top of rice.

3 Moisten top edge of nori sheet with damp fingers. Lift bottom edge and press into rice; roll up. Press gently to seal.

4 Cut rolls into 1-inch slices with sharp knife, wiping knife with warm water if it gets sticky. Place rolls decoratively on platter, cut side up. Serve with pickled ginger and soy sauce.

Sushi Rice

MAKES 2 CUPS (6 TO 8 ROLLS)

1¾ cups water

½ teaspoon salt

1 cup uncooked brown rice or sushi rice

⅓ cup rice vinegar

1 tablespoon sugar

1 teaspoon salt

1 Bring water and salt to a boil in small saucepan. Stir in rice. Reduce heat; simmer, covered, 40 minutes for brown rice or 20 minutes for sushi rice.

2 Remove rice from heat; let stand 5 minutes. Transfer to medium bowl; cool slightly. Stir in vinegar, sugar and salt.

KitchenAid

Thai Seitan Stir-Fry

• • •

1 package (8 ounces) seitan, drained and
thinly sliced

1 jalapeño pepper, halved and seeded

3 cloves garlic

1 (1-inch) piece fresh ginger, peeled

⅓ cup soy sauce

¼ cup packed brown sugar

¼ cup lime juice

½ teaspoon red pepper flakes

¼ teaspoon salt

3 tablespoons vegetable oil

1 medium onion, chopped

2 red bell peppers, quartered
and thinly sliced

2 cups fresh broccoli florets

3 green onions, sliced diagonally

4 cups lightly packed baby spinach

3 cups hot cooked rice

¼ cup shredded fresh basil

¼ cup salted peanuts, chopped

MAKES 4 TO 6 SERVINGS

1 Place seitan slices in medium bowl. Combine jalapeño, garlic and ginger in food processor; process until finely chopped. Add soy sauce, brown sugar, lime juice, red pepper flakes and salt; process until blended. Pour mixture over seitan; toss to coat. Marinate at least 20 minutes at room temperature.

2 Heat oil in wok or large skillet over high heat. Add onion, bell peppers and broccoli. Stir-fry 3 to 5 minutes. Add seitan, marinade and green onions. Bring to a boil; stir-fry 3 minutes or until vegetables are crisp-tender and seitan is hot. Add spinach in two additions, stirring until beginning to wilt after each addition.

3 Serve over rice; sprinkle with basil and peanuts.

KitchenAid

Sesame Ginger-Glazed Tofu with Rice

• • •

1 package (14 ounces)
extra firm tofu

1 cup sesame ginger stir-fry
sauce, divided

1 cup uncooked long grain rice

4 medium carrots, chopped
(about 1 cup)

4 ounces snow peas, halved
(about 1 cup)

MAKES 4 SERVINGS

1 Slice tofu in half crosswise. Cut each half into two triangles. Place tofu
triangles on cutting board between layers of paper towels. Place another
cutting board on top to press moisture out of tofu. Let stand about
15 minutes.

2 Spread ½ cup stir-fry sauce in baking dish. Add tofu; marinate at room
temperature 30 minutes, turning after 15 minutes.

3 Meanwhile, cook rice according to package directions. Keep warm.

4 Spray indoor grill pan with nonstick cooking spray; heat over medium-
high heat. Place tofu in pan; grill 6 to 8 minutes or until lightly browned,
turning once.

5 Meanwhile, pour remaining ½ cup stir-fry sauce into large nonstick
skillet; heat over medium-high heat. Add carrots and snow peas; sauté 4 to
6 minutes or until crisp-tender. Stir in rice; serve with tofu.

Edamame **Frittata**

● ● ●

2 tablespoons olive oil

½ cup frozen shelled edamame

⅓ cup corn

¼ cup chopped shallot

5 eggs

¾ teaspoon Italian seasoning

½ teaspoon salt

½ teaspoon freshly ground black pepper

¼ cup chopped green onions

½ cup crumbled goat cheese

MAKES 4 SERVINGS

1 Preheat broiler. Heat olive oil in large ovenproof skillet over medium-high heat. Add edamame, corn and shallot; sauté 6 to 8 minutes or until shallot is browned and edamame is hot.

2 Meanwhile, beat eggs, Italian seasoning, salt and pepper in medium bowl. Stir in green onions. Pour egg mixture over vegetables in skillet. Sprinkle with cheese. Cook over medium heat 5 to 7 minutes or until eggs are set on bottom, lifting up mixture to allow uncooked portion to flow underneath.

3 Broil 6 inches from heat about 1 minute or until top is puffy and golden. Loosen frittata from skillet with spatula; slide onto plate. Cut into wedges to serve.

KitchenAid

Chickpea Vegetable Curry

• • •

1 tablespoon olive or canola oil

1 large onion, chopped

1 teaspoon minced garlic

1 tablespoon curry powder

1 can (about 12 ounces) evaporated milk plus 1 can water

½ teaspoon salt

¼ teaspoon coconut extract

1½ cups sliced carrots

2 cups cubed peeled potatoes

1 can (about 15 ounces) chickpeas, rinsed and drained

1 cup fresh or frozen cut green beans

6 cups cooked rice

Toppings: chutney, chopped peanuts, golden raisins and chopped green onions

MAKES 6 SERVINGS

1 Heat oil in large saucepan over medium-high heat. Add onion; sauté 5 minutes or until soft. Add garlic; sauté 1 minute. Stir in curry powder.

2 Add evaporated milk, water, salt and coconut extract. Bring to a boil. Add carrots; cook 10 minutes, stirring occasionally.

3 Add potatoes; cook 10 minutes, stirring occasionally. Add chickpeas; cook 10 minutes.

4 Stir in green beans; cook 5 minutes or until vegetables are tender. Serve over rice with desired toppings.

Portobello **and Fontina Sandwiches**

• • •

1 tablespoon olive oil, divided

2 large portobello mushrooms, stems removed

Salt and freshly ground black pepper

2 to 3 tablespoons sun-dried tomato pesto

4 slices crusty Italian bread

4 ounces fontina cheese, sliced

½ cup fresh basil leaves

Additional olive oil

MAKES 2 SERVINGS

1 Preheat broiler. Line baking sheet with foil.

2 Drizzle 2 teaspoons oil over both sides of mushrooms; season with salt and pepper. Place mushrooms, gill sides up, on prepared baking sheet. Broil mushrooms 4 minutes per side or until tender. Cut into ¼-inch-thick slices.

3 Spread pesto evenly over two bread slices; layer with mushrooms, cheese and basil. Top with remaining bread slices. Brush outsides of sandwiches lightly with remaining 1 teaspoon olive oil.

4 Heat large grill pan or skillet over medium heat. Add sandwiches; press down lightly with spatula or weigh down with small plate. Cook 5 minutes on each side or until cheese is melted and sandwiches are golden brown.

KitchenAid

Savory **Stuffed Tomatoes**

• • •

2 large ripe tomatoes
(1 to 1¼ pounds)

¾ cup garlic croutons

¼ cup chopped pitted kalamata olives
2 tablespoons chopped fresh basil

1 clove garlic, minced

¼ cup grated Parmesan or Romano
cheese

1 tablespoon olive oil

¼ teaspoon salt

MAKES 2 SERVINGS

1 Preheat oven to 425°F. Cut tomatoes in half crosswise; discard seeds. Scrape out and reserve pulp. Place tomato shells, cut side up, in pie plate or pan; set aside.

2 Chop tomato pulp; place in medium bowl. Add croutons, olives, basil and garlic; mix well. Spoon mixture into tomato shells. Sprinkle with cheese and drizzle with olive oil.

3 Bake about 10 minutes or until heated through. Season with salt.

Spinach and Mushroom Enchiladas

• • •

2 packages (10 ounces each) frozen chopped spinach, thawed and drained

1½ cups sliced mushrooms

1 can (about 15 ounces) pinto beans, rinsed and drained

3 teaspoons chili powder, divided

¼ teaspoon red pepper flakes

1 can (about 8 ounces) tomato sauce

2 tablespoons water

½ teaspoon hot pepper sauce

8 (8-inch) corn tortillas

1 cup (4 ounces) shredded Monterey Jack cheese

Shredded lettuce, chopped tomatoes, sour cream and chopped fresh cilantro (optional)

MAKES 4 SERVINGS

1 Preheat oven to 350°F. Combine spinach, mushrooms, beans, 2 teaspoons chili powder and red pepper flakes in large skillet; sauté over medium heat 5 minutes.

2 Combine tomato sauce, water, remaining 1 teaspoon chili powder and hot pepper sauce in medium skillet. Dip tortillas into tomato sauce mixture; stack tortillas on waxed paper.

3 Spoon spinach filling onto center of tortillas; roll up, securing with toothpicks if necessary, and place in 11×8-inch baking dish. Spread remaining tomato sauce mixture over enchiladas. Top with cheese.

4 Bake 30 minutes or until heated through and cheese is melted. Serve with lettuce, tomatoes, sour cream and cilantro, if desired.

Black Bean Cakes

• • •

1 can (about 15 ounces) black beans, rinsed and drained

¼ cup all-purpose flour

¼ cup chopped fresh cilantro

2 tablespoons plain yogurt or sour cream

1 tablespoon chili powder

2 cloves garlic, minced

1 tablespoon oil

Salsa

Spanish-style rice (optional)

MAKES 4 SERVINGS

1 Place beans in medium bowl; mash with fork or potato masher until almost smooth, leaving some beans in larger pieces. Stir in flour, cilantro, yogurt, chili powder and garlic. Shape bean mixture into eight patties.

2 Heat oil in large nonstick skillet over medium-high heat. Cook patties 6 to 8 minutes or until lightly browned, turning once. Serve with salsa and rice, if desired.

Onion, Cheese and Tomato Tart

• • •

2 cups all-purpose flour, divided

¼ cup grated Parmesan cheese

1 tablespoon sugar

1 package (¼ ounce) active dry yeast

1 teaspoon salt

½ teaspoon freshly ground black pepper, plus additional for serving

⅔ cup warm water (105° to 115°F)

1 tablespoon olive oil

1 tablespoon butter

1 medium onion, thinly sliced

1 cup (4 ounces) shredded Swiss cheese

2 to 3 ripe tomatoes, sliced

2 tablespoons chopped fresh chives

MAKES 6 TO 8 SERVINGS

1 Combine 1¾ cups flour, Parmesan cheese, sugar, yeast, salt and ½ teaspoon pepper in bowl of stand mixer. Stir in water and oil on low until rough dough forms. Knead on low 5 to 7 minutes or until dough is smooth and elastic, adding remaining ¼ cup flour if necessary. Shape dough into ball. Place in large greased bowl; turn to grease top. Cover and let rise in warm place 1 hour or until doubled.

2 Meanwhile, melt butter in large skillet over medium heat. Add onion; sauté 20 minutes or until tender.

3 Punch down dough. Knead on lightly floured surface 1 minute or until smooth. Flatten into disc. Roll dough into 11-inch round. Press onto bottom and up side of buttered 9- or 10-inch tart pan with removable bottom. Spread onion over dough; sprinkle with Swiss cheese. Let rise in warm place 20 to 30 minutes or until edges are puffy.

4 Preheat oven to 400°F. Layer tomatoes over onion; sprinkle with additional pepper. Bake 25 minutes or until edges are deep golden and cheese is melted. Let cool 10 minutes. Transfer to serving platter. Sprinkle with chives. Cut into wedges.

KitchenAid

sides and salads

Butternut Squash Purée
with Glazed Pecans

• • • •

1 egg white

¼ cup maple syrup, divided

1 tablespoon packed brown sugar

½ teaspoon salt, divided

¼ teaspoon ground cinnamon

2 cups pecan halves

1 (2-pound) butternut squash

1 tablespoon butter

1 large shallot, chopped

2 tablespoons heavy cream

¼ teaspoon freshly ground black pepper

Pinch ground allspice

MAKES 4 SERVINGS

1 Preheat oven to 300°F. Line large baking sheet with foil; grease foil.

2 For pecans, beat egg white in bowl of stand mixer on medium until frothy. Add 2 tablespoons maple syrup, brown sugar, ¼ teaspoon salt and cinnamon; beat until well blended. Add pecans; stir with spatula until evenly coated. Spread pecans on prepared baking sheet.

3 Bake 30 minutes, turning once or twice. Cool on baking sheet 5 minutes, stirring occasionally to prevent sticking; set aside. *Increase oven temperature to 350°F.*

4 Meanwhile, for purée, pierce squash in several places. Microwave 11 to 12 minutes on HIGH or until knife inserted into thickest part comes out easily and squash feels slightly tender to the touch.* Set aside until squash is cool enough to handle.

5 Melt butter in small saucepan over medium heat. Add shallot; cook and stir 2 to 3 minutes or until tender. Cut squash in half and discard seeds and stringy flesh. Scoop out squash flesh; place in blender. Add shallot, cream, remaining 2 tablespoons maple syrup, remaining ¼ teaspoon salt, pepper and allspice; blend until smooth. Spread in shallow baking dish.

6 Bake 15 minutes or until heated through. Sprinkle with ½ cup pecans before serving.

TIP: Store leftover pecans in an airtight container at room temperature. Sprinkle over oatmeal or salads, add to cookies or granola, or eat as a snack.

*To cook on stovetop, bring large saucepan of water to a boil. Quarter and seed squash; place squash in boiling water, adding additional water if needed to cover squash. Cook 30 minutes or until tender. Drain well; set aside until squash is cool enough to handle.

KitchenAid

Rustic Garlic **Mashed Potatoes**

• • •

2 pounds unpeeled baking potatoes,
cut into ½-inch cubes

¼ cup water

2 tablespoons butter,
cut into pieces

1¼ teaspoons salt

½ teaspoon garlic powder

¼ teaspoon freshly ground black pepper

1 cup milk, warmed

MAKES 5 SERVINGS

1 Place all ingredients except milk in slow cooker; toss to combine. Cover; cook on LOW 7 hours or on HIGH 4 hours.

2 Add milk to potatoes. Mash potatoes with potato masher or electric mixer until smooth.

KitchenAid

Mexican-Style **Corn on the Cob (Elotes)**

● ● ●

¼ cup mayonnaise

1 teaspoon chili powder

1 teaspoon grated lime peel

1 clove garlic, minced

4 ears corn, shucked

¼ cup grated Cojita or Parmesan cheese

MAKES 4 SERVINGS

1 Prepare grill for direct cooking. Combine mayonnaise, chili powder, lime peel and garlic in small bowl.

2 Grill corn 4 to 6 minutes or until lightly charred, turning several times. Immediately spread mayonnaise mixture over corn. Sprinkle with cheese.

Orange- and Maple-Glazed **Roasted Beets**

• • •

4 medium beets, scrubbed

2 teaspoons olive oil

2 teaspoons grated orange peel, divided

¼ cup freshly squeezed orange juice

3 tablespoons balsamic or cider vinegar

2 tablespoons maple syrup

1 teaspoon Dijon mustard

1 to 2 tablespoons chopped fresh mint (optional)

MAKES 4 SERVINGS

1 Preheat oven to 425°F.

2 Rub beets with olive oil; place in baking dish. Cover and bake 45 minutes to 1 hour or until knife inserted into largest beet goes in easily. Let stand until cool enough to handle. Peel beets and cut into wedges.

3 Return beets to baking dish. Combine 1 teaspoon orange peel, orange juice, vinegar, maple syrup and mustard in small bowl. Pour over beets. Bake 10 to 15 minutes or until beets are heated through. Remove from oven; arrange on serving platter. Sprinkle with remaining orange peel and mint, if desired.

Lemon-Mint **Red Potatoes**

• • •

2 pounds new red potatoes

3 tablespoons olive oil

1 teaspoon salt

¾ teaspoon dried Greek seasoning or dried oregano

¼ teaspoon garlic powder

¼ teaspoon freshly ground black pepper

1 teaspoon grated lemon peel

2 tablespoons lemon juice

2 tablespoons butter

4 tablespoons chopped fresh mint, divided

MAKES 4 SERVINGS

1 Coat 6-quart slow cooker with nonstick cooking spray. Add potatoes and oil, stirring gently to coat. Sprinkle with salt, Greek seasoning, garlic powder and pepper. Cover; cook on LOW 7 hours or on HIGH 4 hours.

2 Stir in lemon peel, lemon juice, butter and 2 tablespoons mint until butter is completely melted. Cover; cook on HIGH 15 minutes to allow flavors to blend. Sprinkle with remaining 2 tablespoons mint just before serving.

Rustic Dried **Cherry Salad**

• • •

3 cups French bread cubes

¼ cup pecans, chopped

½ cup dried sweetened cherries, chopped

1 stalk celery, diced

3 tablespoons canola oil

3 tablespoons raspberry vinegar

1 tablespoon honey

2 tablespoons water

¼ teaspoon curry powder

MAKES 4 SERVINGS

1 Preheat oven to 350°F. Spread bread cubes on baking sheet; bake 15 minutes or until toasted. Transfer to wire rack; cool completely.

2 Spread pecans on baking sheet. Bake 3 to 5 minutes or until toasted, stirring occasionally. Cool completely.

3 Combine pecans, cherries, celery and bread in large bowl.

4 Whisk oil, vinegar, honey, water and curry powder in small bowl. Pour over salad; toss. Serve immediately.

Zesty **Zucchini-Chickpea Salad**

• • •

3 medium zucchini

½ teaspoon salt

5 tablespoons white vinegar

1 clove garlic, minced

¼ teaspoon dried thyme

½ cup olive oil

1 cup drained canned chickpeas

½ cup sliced pitted ripe olives

3 green onions, minced

1 canned chipotle pepper in adobo sauce, seeded and minced

1 ripe avocado, cut into ½-inch cubes

⅓ cup crumbled feta chese

1 head Boston lettuce, separated into leaves

Sliced tomatoes and fresh cilantro leaves (optional)

MAKES 4 TO 6 SERVINGS

1 Cut zucchini lengthwise into halves; cut halves crosswise into ¼-inch-thick slices. Place slices in medium bowl; sprinkle with salt; toss to mix. Spread zucchini on several layers of paper towels. Let stand at room temperature 30 minutes to drain.

2 Combine vinegar, garlic and thyme in large bowl. Gradually add oil, whisking constantly until thoroughly blended.

3 Pat zucchini dry; add to dressing. Add chickpeas, olives and onions; toss lightly to coat. Cover and refrigerate at least 30 minutes or up to 4 hours, stirring occasionally.

4 Add chipotle, avocado and cheese just before serving. Stir gently. Serve on lettuce with tomatoes and cilantro, if desired.

Spinach Salad
with Orange Chili-Glazed Shrimp

• • •

¾ cup orange juice, divided

5 cloves garlic, minced, divided

1 teaspoon chili powder

8 ounces large shrimp, peeled and deveined (with tails on)

2 teaspoons sesame seeds

1 tablespoon cider vinegar

1 teaspoon grated orange peel

1 teaspoon olive oil

½ teaspoon honey

⅛ teaspoon red pepper flakes

12 cups baby spinach

1 large ripe mango, peeled and cubed

½ cup crumbled feta cheese

MAKES 4 SERVINGS

1 Combine ½ cup orange juice, 4 cloves garlic and chili powder in large nonstick skillet. Bring to a boil over high heat. Boil 3 minutes or until mixture reduces and just coats bottom of skillet.

2 Reduce heat to medium. Add shrimp; sauté 2 minutes or until shrimp are opaque and glazed. Add additional orange juice or water to keep shrimp moist, if necessary.

3 Heat small nonstick skillet over medium heat. Add sesame seeds; cook about 4 minutes or until golden, stirring frequently. Transfer to small bowl. Whisk in remaining ¼ cup orange juice, vinegar, remaining 1 clove garlic, orange peel, olive oil, honey and red pepper flakes.

4 Place spinach in large bowl; drizzle with some of dressing and toss to coat. Top with mango, cheese and shrimp; drizzle with remaining dressing.

Tuna and Fennel **Pasta Salad**

• • •

Balsamic Vinaigrette
(recipe follows)

¾ pound yellow fin tuna steaks

2 teaspoons Dijon mustard

8 ounces uncooked small pasta shells,
cooked and cooled

4 cups torn red leaf lettuce

2 cups cut asparagus spears, cooked
crisp-tender and cooled

½ cup thinly sliced fennel

½ cup thinly sliced red bell pepper

8 cherry tomatoes, halved

Salt and freshly ground black pepper

MAKES 4 SERVINGS

1 Prepare Balsamic Vinaigrette. Prepare grill for direct cooking.*

2 Brush tuna with mustard. Grill tuna over medium heat coals about 5 minutes on each side or until fish is tender and flakes easily when tested with fork. Break into chunks.

3 Toss tuna, pasta, lettuce, asparagus, fennel, bell pepper and tomatoes in large bowl; drizzle with vinaigrette and toss. Season with salt and black pepper.

Balsamic Vinaigrette

¼ cup balsamic vinegar

¼ cup water

3 tablespoons olive oil

2 tablespoons finely chopped red onion

3 cloves garlic, minced

¾ teaspoon dried chervil

½ teaspoon celery seed

Combine all ingredients in jar with tight-fitting lid; refrigerate until ready to serve. Shake well before using.

Or preheat broiler. Broil tuna 6 inches from heat source 5 minutes on each side.

KitchenAid

Spinach-Melon Salad

• • •

6 cups packed torn stemmed spinach

4 cups mixed melon balls (cantaloupe,
honeydew and watermelon)

1 cup zucchini ribbons*

½ cup sliced red bell pepper

¼ cup thinly sliced red onion

¼ cup red wine vinegar

2 tablespoons honey

2 teaspoons olive oil

2 teaspoons lime juice

1 teaspoon poppy seeds

1 teaspoon dried mint

*To make ribbons, thinly slice zucchini
lengthwise with vegetable peeler.

MAKES 6 SERVINGS

1 Combine spinach, melon, zucchini, bell pepper and onion in large bowl.

2 Combine vinegar, honey, oil, lime juice, poppy seeds and mint in small jar with tight-fitting lid; shake well. Pour over salad; toss gently to coat.

KitchenAid

Mesclun Salad with Cranberry Vinaigrette

• • •

⅓ cup extra virgin olive oil

3 tablespoons champagne vinegar or sherry vinegar

1 tablespoon Dijon mustard

¾ teaspoon salt

¼ teaspoon freshly ground black pepper

½ cup dried cranberries

10 cups (10 ounces) packed mesclun or mixed torn salad greens

4 ounces goat cheese, crumbled

½ cup walnuts or pecans, coarsely chopped and toasted*

To toast nuts, spread in single layer on baking sheet. Bake in preheated 350°F oven 8 to 10 minutes or until golden brown, stirring frequently.

MAKES 8 SERVINGS

1 For dressing, whisk oil, vinegar, mustard, salt and pepper in medium bowl. Stir in cranberries. Cover; refrigerate at least 30 minutes or up to 24 hours before serving.

2 For salad, combine greens, goat cheese and walnuts in large bowl. Whisk dressing and pour over salad; toss until evenly coated.

Couscous with **Carrots and Cranberries**

• • •

2 cups vegetable broth

2 teaspoons olive oil

½ small onion, thinly sliced

½ large carrot, shredded

¼ cup dried cranberries, chopped

¼ teaspoon ground cinnamon

¼ teaspoon ground cumin

¼ teaspoon ground turmeric

1 cup uncooked whole wheat couscous

Salt and freshly ground black pepper

MAKES 4 SERVINGS

1 Bring broth to a boil in medium saucepan; keep warm.

2 Meanwhile, heat oil in medium skillet over medium-low heat. Add onion; sauté about 5 minute or until translucent. Add carrot; sauté 1 minute. Add cranberries; cook 30 seconds. Stir in cinnamon, cumin and turmeric; cook 15 to 20 seconds or until fragrant, stirring constantly.

3 Add vegetable mixture to hot broth; stir in couscous. Season with salt and pepper. Cover; let stand 10 to 15 minutes or until couscous is tender and broth is absorbed. Fluff with fork.

Spinach-Strawberry Salad

• • •

4 ounces slivered almonds

9 ounces baby spinach

¾ cup thinly sliced red onion

⅓ cup pomegranate juice

2 tablespoons dark sesame oil

2 tablespoons vegetable oil

3 tablespoons cider vinegar

3 tablespoons sugar

¼ teaspoon red pepper flakes

⅛ teaspoon salt

2 cups quartered strawberries

4 ounces crumbled goat cheese

MAKES 4 TO 6 SERVINGS

1 Heat medium skillet over medium heat. Add almonds; cook 2 minutes or until beginning to lightly brown, stirring constantly. Transfer to plate; cool completely.

2 Combine spinach and onion in large bowl.

3 Combine pomegranate juice, sesame oil, vegetable oil, vinegar, sugar, red pepper flakes and salt in small jar with tight-fitting lid; shake well. Pour over salad; toss gently to coat. Add strawberries, almonds and goat cheese; toss gently.

Seared Asian **Steak Salad**

● ● ●

12 ounces boneless sirloin steak,
¾-inch thick

2 tablespoons soy sauce

3 tablespoons hoisin sauce*

1 teaspoon grated orange peel

2 tablespoons fresh orange juice

2 tablespoons cider vinegar

2 tablespoons packed dark
brown sugar

2 teaspoons dark sesame oil

1 teaspoon grated fresh ginger

⅛ teaspoon red pepper flakes

1 package (5 ounces) spring greens

½ cup thinly sliced red onion

1 cup thinly sliced red bell pepper

1 cup snow peas

1 medium carrot, cut into matchstick-size
pieces

2 teaspoons vegetable oil

*Hoisin sauce can be found in the Asian
section of well-stocked supermarkets.*

MAKES 4 SERVINGS

1 Place beef and soy sauce in large resealable food storage bag. Seal bag; turn to coat. Marinate in refrigerator 2 hours or up to 24 hours, turning several times.

2 Whisk hoisin sauce, orange peel, orange juice, vinegar, brown sugar, sesame oil, ginger and red pepper flakes in small bowl. Arrange greens, onion, bell pepper, snow peas and carrots on four serving plates.

3 Remove beef from marinade; discard marinade. Heat vegetable oil in large nonstick skillet over medium heat. Cook beef 6 to 8 minutes or until desired doneness, turning once. Transfer beef to cutting board; let stand 3 minutes before thinly slicing.

4 Whisk dressing; drizzle over salads. Top each salad with beef.

Spinach Salad with Stuffed Mushrooms

• • •

¼ cup olive oil

3 tablespoons balsamic vinegar

2 teaspoons chopped shallots

¼ teaspoon salt

8 cremini mushrooms, stemmed

2 teaspoons honey

4 ounces herbed goat cheese, softened

2 tablespoons cream cheese, softened

5 ounces baby spinach

¼ cup sliced almonds

MAKES 4 SERVINGS

1 Whisk olive oil, vinegar, shallots and salt in small bowl. Place mushrooms in baking dish, gill sides up. Drizzle 2 tablespoons oil mixture over mushrooms; marinate 15 to 30 minutes. Whisk honey into remaining oil mixture; set aside.

2 Preheat oven to 400°F. Combine goat cheese and cream cheese in small bowl; set aside to soften.

3 Turn mushrooms cap sides up. Bake 10 minutes. Turn mushrooms over. Stuff each mushroom with about 1 tablespoon goat cheese mixture. Bake 5 to 10 minutes or until cheese is warm and soft. Transfer to plate. Whisk cooking liquid into dressing.

4 Arrange spinach in large bowl or on individual serving plates. Drizzle with half of dressing; toss to coat. Top with stuffed mushrooms; drizzle with remaining dressing and sprinkle with almonds.

cookies, brownies and bars

Chocolate Chip Shortbread
with Earl Grey Glaze

• • •

1 cup (2 sticks) butter

½ cup sugar

1 teaspoon grated orange peel

2 cups all-purpose flour

¼ cup cornstarch

¼ teaspoon salt

½ cup miniature chocolate chips

Earl Grey-Infused Glaze
(recipe follows)

MAKES ABOUT 2½ DOZEN COOKIES

1 Preheat oven to 300°F.

2 Beat butter, sugar and orange peel in bowl of stand mixer on medium speed until well blended. Gradually beat in flour, cornstarch and salt on low just until dough forms. Stir in chocolate chips on low until combined.

3 Roll dough into ¼-inch-thick rectangle on lightly floured surface. Cut dough into 32 squares or rectangles with knife or pizza cutter. Place 1 inch apart on ungreased baking sheets.

4 Bake 20 to 25 minutes or until bottoms are lightly browned. Cool on cookie sheets 5 minutes. Remove to wire racks to cool completely.

5 Prepare Earl Grey Glaze. Drizzle over shortbread.

Earl Grey Glaze

¼   **cup boiling water**

3   **bags Earl Grey tea**

1   **cup powdered sugar**

1   **tablespoon butter, softened**

1 Pour boiling water over tea bags; let steep 3 to 5 minutes. Remove tea bags.

2 Mix powdered sugar and butter in small bowl. Gradually stir in enough tea until glaze is desired consistency.

Lemon Drops

• • •

2 cups all-purpose flour

⅛ teaspoon salt

1 cup (2 sticks) butter, softened

1 cup powdered sugar, divided

2 teaspoons lemon juice

Grated peel of 1 lemon (about 1½ teaspoons)

MAKES ABOUT 6 DOZEN COOKIES

1 Preheat oven to 300°F.

2 Combine flour and salt in medium bowl. Beat butter and ¾ cup powdered sugar in bowl of stand mixer on medium until fluffy. Beat in lemon juice and peel until well blended. Add flour mixture, ½ cup at a time, beating just until blended.

3 Shape rounded teaspoonfuls of dough into balls. Place 1 inch apart on ungreased cookie sheets.

4 Bake 20 to 25 minutes or until bottoms are lightly browned. Cool on cookie sheets 5 minutes. Remove to wire racks to cool completely. Sprinkle with remaining ¼ cup powdered sugar.

Macadamia Chocolate Chunk Cookies
● ● ●

1 cup packed brown sugar

¾ cup granulated sugar

1 cup (2 sticks) butter, softened

2 eggs

2 teaspoons vanilla

2½ cups all-purpose flour, divided

½ cup unsweetened cocoa powder

1 teaspoon baking powder

½ teaspoon salt

1 package (8 ounces) semisweet baking chocolate, cut into small chunks

1 jar (3½ ounces) macadamia nuts, coarsely chopped

MAKES 4 DOZEN COOKIES

1 Preheat oven to 325°F. Grease cookie sheets.

2 Combine brown sugar, granulated sugar and butter in bowl of stand mixer. Beat on medium-high 3 to 5 minutes or until light and fluffy. Beat in eggs and vanilla.

3 Add 1 cup flour, cocoa powder, baking powder and salt. Mix on low about 30 seconds. Gradually beat in remaining 1½ cups flour on low. Add chocolate chunks and nuts; mix on low just until blended. Drop rounded teaspoonfuls of dough 2 inches apart onto prepared cookie sheets.

4 Bake 12 to 13 minutes or until edges are set. Do not overbake. Cool on cookie sheets about 1 minute. Remove to wire racks to cool completely.

Coconut Almond Biscotti

• • •

2½ cups all-purpose flour

1⅓ cups flaked coconut

¾ cup sliced almonds

⅔ cup sugar

2 teaspoons baking powder

½ teaspoon salt

½ cup (1 stick) butter, melted

1 egg, at room temperature

1 egg white, at room temperature

1 teaspoon vanilla

MAKES ABOUT 2 DOZEN BISCOTTI

1 Preheat oven to 350°F. Line cookie sheet with parchment paper.

2 Combine flour, coconut, almonds, sugar, baking powder and salt in bowl of stand mixer. Mix on low 1 minute or until combined.

3 Whisk butter, egg, egg white and vanilla in medium bowl until well blended. Gradually add butter mixture to flour mixture on low until blended.

4 Divide dough into two pieces. Shape each piece into 8×3×¾-inch loaf with floured hands. Place 3 inches apart on prepared cookie sheet.

5 Bake 26 to 28 minutes or until golden and set. Cool on cookie sheet 10 minutes. Transfer to wire rack. Slice each loaf diagonally into ½-inch-thick slices with serrated knife. Place slices, cut sides down, on cookie sheet.

6 Bake 20 minutes or until firm and golden. Remove to wire rack to cool completely.

Maple Walnut Finger Cookies

● ● ●

¾ cup (1½ sticks) butter, softened

¾ cup granulated sugar

3 egg yolks

3 tablespoons plus 1 teaspoon maple extract, divided

2 cups all-purpose flour

¾ cup finely chopped walnuts

¼ teaspoon salt

2½ cups powdered sugar

MAKES 3½ DOZEN COOKIES

1 Beat butter and granulated sugar in bowl of stand mixer on medium 1 minute or until light and fluffy. Beat in egg yolks and 1 teaspoon maple extract until well blended. Add flour, walnuts and salt; beat on low just until combined. Divide dough in half. Shape each half into 6×3×1-inch rectangles. Wrap in plastic wrap; refrigerate at least 2 hours or overnight.

2 Preheat oven to 375°F. Line cookie sheets with parchment paper. Cut dough into ¼-inch slices; place 1 inch apart on prepared cookie sheets.

3 Bake 12 to 14 minutes or until edges are light brown. Cool on cookie sheets 5 minutes.

4 Whisk powdered sugar and remaining 3 tablespoons maple extract in small bowl until smooth. Dip half of each cookie into icing; place on parchment or waxed paper. Let stand until cookies are cool and icing is set.

Soft Ginger Cookies

• • •

2 cups all-purpose flour

1½ teaspoons ground ginger

1 teaspoon baking soda

¼ teaspoon salt

¼ teaspoon ground cinnamon

¼ teaspoon ground cloves

¼ cup packed brown sugar

¼ cup canola oil

¼ cup molasses

½ cup sour cream

1 egg white

MAKES ABOUT 2½ DOZEN COOKIES

1 Preheat oven to 350°F.

2 Combine flour, ginger, baking soda, salt, cinnamon and cloves in large bowl. Beat brown sugar, oil and molasses in bowl of stand mixer on medium 1 minute or until smooth. Add sour cream and egg white; beat until well blended. Gradually add flour mixture, beating on low until well blended.

3 Drop rounded tablespoonfuls of dough 2 inches apart onto ungreased cookie sheets. Flatten dough to ⅛-inch thickness with bottom of glass lightly sprayed with nonstick cooking spray.

4 Bake 10 minutes or until tops of cookies puff up and spring back when lightly touched. Cool on cookie sheets 2 minutes. Remove to wire racks to cool completely.

KitchenAid

Peanut Butter Cookies

• • •

½ cup peanut butter

½ cup (1 stick) butter, softened

½ cup granulated sugar

½ cup packed brown sugar

1 egg

½ teaspoon vanilla

1¼ cups all-purpose flour

½ teaspoon baking soda

¼ teaspoon salt

MAKES 3 DOZEN COOKIES

1 Preheat oven to 375°F.

2 Combine peanut butter and butter in bowl of stand mixer; beat on medium-high 1 minute or until smooth. Add granulated sugar, brown sugar, egg and vanilla; beat on medium about 1 minute. Gradually add flour, baking soda and salt on low; mix 30 seconds.

3 Roll dough into 1-inch balls. Place balls about 2 inches apart on ungreased cookie sheets. Press with fork in crisscross pattern to ¼-inch thickness.

4 Bake 10 to 12 minutes or until golden brown. Remove to wire racks to cool completely.

Chocolate Chip Cookies

• • •

1 cup granulated sugar

1 cup packed brown sugar

1 cup (2 sticks) butter, softened

2 eggs

1½ teaspoons vanilla

1 teaspoon baking soda

1 teaspoon salt

3 cups all-purpose flour

1 package (12 ounces) semisweet chocolate chips, divided

MAKES ABOUT 4½ DOZEN COOKIES

1 Preheat oven to 375°F. Line cookie sheets with parchment paper.

2 Combine granulated sugar, brown sugar and butter in bowl of stand mixer; beat on medium-high 3 to 5 minutes or until light and fluffy. Beat in eggs and vanilla. Beat in baking soda and salt on low. Gradually add flour on low; mix 30 seconds. Stir in 1½ cups chips on low.

3 Drop rounded teaspoonfuls of dough 2 inches apart onto prepared cookie sheets. Press 2 to 4 remaining chocolate chips into each cookie.

4 Bake 10 to 12 minutes or until edges are lightly browned. Remove to wire racks to cool completely.

KitchenAid

Brown Edge Wafers

• • •

½ cup (1 stick) butter, softened

½ cup sugar

1 egg

1 teaspoon vanilla

½ teaspoon grated orange peel

1 cup all-purpose flour

Melted chocolate

MAKES 2 DOZEN COOKIES

1 Preheat oven to 375°F. Line cookie sheets with parchment paper.

2 Combine butter and sugar in bowl of stand mixer; beat on high 30 seconds or until well blended. Add egg, vanilla and orange peel; beat on high 30 seconds or until fluffy. Add flour on low, mixing 15 seconds or just until blended. Drop teaspoonfuls of dough 2 inches apart onto prepared cookie sheets.

3 Bake 8 to 10 minutes or until edges are lightly browned. Remove to wire racks to cool completely. Drizzle with melted chocolate.

Pecan Shortbread Cookies

• • •

1 cup (2 sticks) butter

¾ cup packed brown sugar

1 teaspoon vanilla

2½ cups all-purpose flour

½ cup chopped pecans

MAKES 2 DOZEN COOKIES

1 Combine butter, brown sugar and vanilla in bowl of stand mixer. Beat on medium-high 1 minute. Stop and scrape bowl. Gradually add flour on low; beat 30 seconds. Add pecans, mixing just until blended.

2 Shape dough into 1½-inch-diameter log. Wrap in waxed paper; refrigerate 20 minutes.

3 Preheat oven to 325°F. Grease cookie sheets or line with parchment paper. Slice dough into ½-inch-thick rounds. Place on prepared cookie sheets. Bake 18 to 20 minutes or until cookies are firm. Remove to wire racks to cool completely.

○ **TIP**

STORE SOFT COOKIES BETWEEN LAYERS OF WAXED PAPER IN AN AIRTIGHT CONTAINER. A PIECE OF APPLE OR BREAD, CHANGED FREQUENTLY, WILL HELP KEEP COOKIES SOFT. STORE CRISP COOKIES IN AN AIRTIGHT CONTAINER WITH A LOOSE-FITTING LID. IF THEY SOFTEN, PLACE THEM IN A 300°F OVEN FOR 3 TO 5 MINUTES BEFORE SERVING.

KitchenAid

Coconut-Lemon Layer Bars

• • •

2 cups vanilla wafer crumbs

6 tablespoons butter, melted

1 package (8 ounces) cream cheese, softened

1 tablespoon grated lemon peel

3 tablespoons fresh lemon juice

1 egg

1 cup (6 ounces) white chocolate chips

1 cup flaked coconut

½ cup chopped macadamia nuts

MAKES ABOUT 2 DOZEN BARS

1 Preheat oven to 350°F. Combine vanilla wafer crumbs and butter in medium bowl; stir until well blended. Press mixture firmly in bottom of 13×9-inch baking pan.

2 Beat cream cheese, lemon peel, lemon juice and egg in bowl of stand mixer on low until smooth. Spread evenly over crumb mixture. Sprinkle white chocolate chips, coconut and nuts over cream cheese layer; press firmly with fork.

3 Bake 25 to 30 minutes or until lightly browned. Cool completely in pan on wire rack. Cut into bars.

Key Lime Bars

• • •

1½ cups finely crushed graham crackers (about 10 to 12 crackers)

¼ cup packed brown sugar

5 tablespoons melted butter

2 tablespoons all-purpose flour

1 package (8 ounces) cream cheese, softened

1½ cups granulated sugar

2 eggs

¼ cup fresh key lime juice

1 tablespoon grated lime peel

MAKES ABOUT 2 DOZEN BARS

1 Preheat oven to 350°F. Grease 13×9-inch baking pan.

2 Combine graham cracker crumbs, brown sugar, butter and flour in large bowl; stir until well blended. Press mixture firmly in bottom of prepared pan. Bake 15 minutes.

3 Beat cream cheese and granulated sugar in bowl of stand mixer on medium until smooth and creamy. Add eggs; beat until blended. Stir in lime juice and lime peel. Pour filling over warm crust.

4 Bake 15 to 20 minutes or until filling is set. Cool in pan on wire rack 2 hours. Cut into bars with sharp knife. If filling sticks to knife, dip blade into warm water and wipe clean before each slice.

KitchenAid

Orange Marmalade Bars

• • •

¾ cup hazelnuts, toasted and skins
removed,* divided

1 cup plus 1 teaspoon all-purpose flour,
divided

¼ cup plus 2 tablespoons packed
brown sugar, divided

6 tablespoons cold butter, cut into pieces

1 egg

1 teaspoon vanilla

1 cup plus 2 teaspoons orange
marmalade, divided

4 ounces cream cheese

¼ cup heavy cream

1 tablespoon granulated sugar

1 tablespoon grated
orange peel

2 tablespoons melted butter

*To toast hazelnuts, spread in single
layer on baking sheet. Bake at 350°F
7 minutes or until lightly browned and
fragrant. Place on clean kitchen towel; rub
hazelnuts with towel to remove skins.

MAKES ABOUT 2 DOZEN BARS

1 Preheat oven to 375°F. Grease 13×9-inch baking pan.

2 For crust, place ¼ cup hazelnuts in food processor; process until finely ground. Transfer to bowl of stand mixer; whisk in 1 cup flour and ¼ cup brown sugar. Scatter cold butter over flour mixture; mix on low 1 minute or until coarse crumbs form. Add egg and vanilla; mix on low until dough forms. Press mixture firmly in bottom of prepared pan.

3 Bake 12 to 15 minutes or until crust is golden brown. Spread 1 cup marmalade evenly over hot crust.

4 Combine cream cheese, cream, granulated sugar, remaining 2 teaspoons marmalade and orange peel in bowl of stand mixer. Mix on medium until smooth and creamy. Finely chop remaining ½ cup hazelnuts; transfer to small bowl. Add remaining 2 tablespoons brown sugar, remaining 1 teaspoon flour and melted butter; toss until nuts are evenly coated. Pour cream cheese mixture over marmalade and crust. Sprinkle hazelnut topping evenly over filling.

5 Bake 12 to 15 minutes or until topping is lightly browned and filling bubbles slightly. Cool in pan on wire rack 2 hours. Cut into bars with sharp knife. If filling sticks to knife, dip blade into warm water and wipe clean before each slice.

Cocoa Brownies

• • •

2 cups all-purpose flour

2 cups granulated sugar

½ cup buttermilk

2 eggs

1 teaspoon baking soda

1 teaspoon vanilla

1 cup (2 sticks) butter

1 cup hot coffee

¼ cup unsweetened cocoa powder

Cocoa Frosting (recipe follows)

MAKES ABOUT 2½ DOZEN BROWNIES

1 Preheat oven to 400°F. Grease 17×11-inch jelly-roll pan.

2 Combine flour and granulated sugar in large bowl. Whisk buttermilk, eggs, baking soda and vanilla in medium bowl until well blended.

3 Combine butter, coffee and cocoa in small heavy saucepan. Bring to a boil over medium heat, stirring constantly. Stir cocoa mixture into flour mixture until smooth. Stir in buttermilk mixture until well blended. Pour batter into prepared pan.

4 Bake 20 minutes or until center springs back when touched. Meanwhile, prepare Cocoa Frosting. Remove brownies from oven; immediately pour warm frosting over hot brownies, spreading evenly. Cool completely in pan on wire rack. Cut into squares.

Cocoa Frosting

½ **cup (1 stick) butter**

¼ **cup milk**

2 **tablespoons unsweetened cocoa powder**

3½ **cups powdered sugar**

1 **teaspoon vanilla**

Combine butter, milk and cocoa in large saucepan; bring to a boil over medium heat. Remove from heat. Stir in powdered sugar and vanilla; beat until smooth.

Peanut Butter-Frosted Brownies

• • •

½ cup water

2 squares (1 ounce each) unsweetened chocolate, cut into pieces

⅓ cup unsweetened cocoa powder, sifted

1 teaspoon vanilla

1⅓ cups all-purpose flour

½ cup packed brown sugar

½ teaspoon baking powder

¼ teaspoon baking soda

¼ teaspoon salt

½ cup mayonnaise

2 eggs

½ cup creamy peanut butter

1 tablespoon granulated sugar

1¼ cups whipped cream

Shaved chocolate (optional)

MAKES 1½ DOZEN BROWNIES

1 Preheat oven to 350°F. Grease 9-inch square baking pan. Place water and chocolate in heavy small saucepan. Heat over low heat, stirring frequently, until chocolate is melted. Remove from heat; stir in cocoa and vanilla. Set aside to cool.

2 Combine flour, brown sugar, baking powder, baking soda and salt in large bowl. Add mayonnaise and eggs; mix well. Add melted chocolate; stir until well blended. Pour batter into prepared pan.

3 Bake 22 to 24 minutes or until toothpick inserted into center comes out clean. Cool completely in pan on wire rack.

4 For frosting, beat peanut butter and granulated sugar in bowl of stand mixer on medium 1 minute. Stir in whipped cream until just blended. Frost brownies; garnish with shaved chocolate.

Whole Wheat Brownies

• • •

½ cup whole wheat flour

½ teaspoon baking soda

¼ teaspoon salt

½ cup (1 stick) butter

1 cup packed brown sugar

½ cup unsweetened cocoa powder

2 eggs

½ cup semisweet chocolate chips

1 teaspoon vanilla

MAKES 1½ DOZEN BROWNIES

1 Preheat oven to 350°F. Grease 8-inch square baking pan. Combine flour, baking soda and salt in small bowl.

2 Melt butter in large saucepan over low heat. Add brown sugar; cook and stir 4 minutes or until sugar is completely dissolved and mixture is smooth. Remove from heat; stir in cocoa until smooth. Add flour mixture; stir until smooth. Beat in eggs. Stir in chocolate chips and vanilla. Spoon batter into prepared pan.

3 Bake 15 to 20 minutes or until toothpick inserted into center comes out almost clean. Cool completely on wire rack. Cut into bars.

Raspberry-Glazed **Brownies**

• • •

3/4 cup all-purpose flour

9 tablespoons granulated sugar, divided

1/4 cup unsweetened cocoa powder

3/4 teaspoon baking powder

1/8 teaspoon salt

1 jar (2 1/2 ounces) prune purée*

1/4 cup cold coffee

1 egg

2 tablespoons canola oil

3/4 teaspoon vanilla, divided

1/4 cup seedless raspberry fruit spread

2 ounces cream cheese, softened

4 1/2 teaspoons milk

Prune purée can be found in the baby food aisle or baking aisle of well-stocked supermarkets.

MAKES 1 DOZEN BROWNIES

1 Preheat oven to 350°F.

2 Combine flour, 7 tablespoons sugar, cocoa, baking powder and salt in large bowl; stir until well blended. Combine prune purée, coffee, egg, oil and 1/2 teaspoon vanilla in medium bowl; stir until well blended. Make well in center of dry ingredients; add prune purée mixture. Stir just until blended.

3 Spread batter evenly into ungreased 8-inch square nonstick baking pan. Bake 8 minutes. (Brownies will not appear to be done.) Cool completely in pan on wire rack.

4 Meanwhile, place raspberry spread in small microwaveable bowl. Microwave on HIGH 10 seconds; stir until smooth. Brush evenly over brownies with pastry brush.

5 Combine cream cheese, milk, remaining 2 tablespoons sugar and remaining 1/4 teaspoon vanilla in bowl of stand mixer. Beat on medium until smooth and well blended.

6 Cut brownies into 12 rectangles; top each with 1 teaspoon cream cheese mixture.

Double-Decker **Butterscotch Brownies**

● ● ●

¾ cup (1½ sticks) butter

2 cups sugar

2 teaspoons vanilla

3 eggs

1 cup all-purpose flour

¾ cup unsweetened cocoa powder

Butterscotch Glaze
(recipe follows)

Chocolate Ganache
(recipe follows)

MAKES 2 DOZEN BARS

1 Preheat oven to 350°F. Line 15×10-inch jelly-roll pan with foil; grease foil.

2 Beat butter, sugar and vanilla in bowl of stand mixer on low 30 seconds or until mixed. Beat on medium-high 2 minutes or until creamy. Add eggs, one at a time, beating well on medium after each addition. Gradually add flour and cocoa on low until blended. Pour batter into prepared pan.

3 Bake 14 to 16 minutes or until top springs back when lightly touched. Cool in pan 2 minutes. Invert onto cutting board and remove foil; invert again onto wire rack. Cool completely.

4 Prepare Butterscotch Glaze. Spread warm glaze evenly over brownies. Cut glazed brownie in half and stack halves, glazed sides up. Let stand until glaze is set. Prepare Chocolate Ganache; drizzle warm ganache over brownies. Let stand until set. Cut into bars.

Butterscotch Glaze

1 package (about 11 ounces) butterscotch baking chips

¼ cup water

¼ cup sugar

1 tablespoon light corn syrup

Place butterscotch chips in bowl of stand mixer. Bring water, sugar and corn syrup to a boil in small saucepan over medium-high heat. Turn mixer to low and slowly pour in hot syrup, mixing until smooth. Cool slightly.

Chocolate Ganache

½ cup heavy cream

1 cup chocolate chips

Heat cream in small saucepan over medium-low heat until bubbles appear around edge of pan. Remove from heat; stir in chocolate chips until smooth. Let stand until slightly thickened.

KitchenAid

Shortbread Turtle Cookie Bars

• • •

1¼ cups (2½ sticks) butter, softened, divided

1 cup all-purpose flour

1 cup old-fashioned oats

1½ cups packed brown sugar, divided

1 teaspoon ground cinnamon

¼ teaspoon salt

1½ cups chopped pecans

6 ounces bittersweet or semisweet chocolate, finely chopped

4 ounces white chocolate, finely chopped

MAKES ABOUT 4 DOZEN BARS

1 Preheat oven to 350°F.

2 Beat ½ cup butter in bowl of stand mixer on medium 2 minutes or until light and fluffy. Add flour, oats, ¾ cup brown sugar, cinnamon and salt; mix on low until coarse crumbs form. Press mixture firmly in bottom of ungreased 13×9-inch baking pan.

3 Heat remaining ¾ cup butter and ¾ cup brown sugar in medium heavy saucepan over medium-high heat, stirring constantly until butter melts. Bring mixture to a boil; cook 1 minute without stirring. Remove from heat; stir in pecans. Pour over crust.

4 Bake 18 to 22 minutes or until caramel begins to bubble. Remove pan from oven. Immediately sprinkle with bittersweet and white chocolates; swirl with knife after 45 seconds to 1 minute or when slightly softened (do not spread). Cool completely in pan on wire rack. Cut into small bars.

KitchenAid

Gooey Caramel Chocolate Bars

• • •

2 cups all-purpose flour

1 cup granulated sugar

¼ teaspoon salt

2 cups (4 sticks) butter, divided

1 cup packed brown sugar

⅓ cup light corn syrup

1 cup semisweet chocolate chips

MAKES 2 DOZEN BARS

1 Preheat oven to 350°F. Line 13×9-inch baking pan with foil.

2 Combine flour, granulated sugar and salt in bowl of stand mixer. Cut 14 tablespoons butter into small pieces; scatter over flour mixture. Mix on low 1 minute or until coarse crumbs form. Press mixture in bottom of prepared pan. Bake 18 to 20 minutes or until lightly browned around edges. Cool completely in pan on wire rack.

3 Combine 1 cup butter, brown sugar and corn syrup in medium heavy saucepan. Cook over medium heat 5 to 8 minutes or until mixture boils, stirring frequently. Boil gently 2 minutes without stirring. Immediately pour over cooled crust; spread evenly to edges of pan. Cool completely.

4 Melt chocolate chips and remaining 2 tablespoons butter in double boiler over hot (not boiling) water. Pour over caramel layer; spread evenly to edges of pan. Refrigerate 10 minutes or until chocolate begins to set. Cool completely. Cut into bars.

cakes and cupcakes

Quick **Yellow Cake**

● ● ●

2¼ cups all-purpose flour

1⅓ cups sugar

3 teaspoons baking powder

½ teaspoon salt

1 cup milk

½ cup shortening

1 teaspoon vanilla

2 eggs

Chocolate Frosting
(recipe follows)

MAKES 10 TO 12 SERVINGS

1 Preheat oven to 350°F. Grease and flour two 8- or 9-inch round cake pans.

2 Combine flour, sugar, baking powder and salt in bowl of stand mixer. Add milk, shortening and vanilla; mix on low about 1 minute. Add eggs; mix on low about 30 seconds. Beat on medium-high about 1 minute. Pour batter into prepared baking pans.

3 Bake 30 to 35 minutes or until toothpick inserted into centers comes out clean. Cool in pans 10 minutes. Remove to wire racks to cool completely.

4 Prepare Chocolate Frosting; fill and frost cake.

Chocolate Frosting

1 cup (2 sticks) butter, softened

2 tablespoons light corn syrup

4 cups powdered sugar

2 ounces unsweetened chocolate, melted

Beat butter in bowl of stand mixer on medium-low about 1 ½ minutes or until creamy. Beat in corn syrup on low until well blended. Gradually add powdered sugar on low, mixing until well blended. Beat on medium about 1 minute. Gradually add melted chocolate on low; mix about 1 ½ minutes. Increase speed to medium; beat about 1 minute.

Molten Cinnamon-**Chocolate Cakes**

● ● ●

6 ounces semisweet chocolate

¾ cup (1½ sticks) butter

1½ cups powdered sugar, plus additional
for garnish

4 eggs

6 tablespoons all-purpose flour

1½ teaspoons vanilla

¾ teaspoon ground cinnamon

Powdered sugar

MAKES 6 CAKES

1 Preheat oven to 425°F. Spray six jumbo muffin cups or six 8-ounce custard cups with nonstick cooking spray.

2 Combine chocolate and butter in medium microwaveable bowl; heat on HIGH 1½ minutes until melted and smooth, stirring every 30 seconds. Whisk in 1½ cups powdered sugar, eggs, flour, vanilla and cinnamon until well blended. Pour batter into prepared muffin cups, filling slightly more than half full.

3 Bake 13 minutes or until cupcakes spring back when lightly touched but centers are soft. Let stand 1 minute; loosen sides with knife. Gently lift out cakes and invert onto serving plates; sprinkle with additional powdered sugar. Serve immediately.

Pumpkin Cheesecake
with Ginger-Pecan Crust

• • •

1¼ cups gingersnap cookie crumbs (about 24 cookies)

⅓ cup pecans, very finely chopped

¼ cup granulated sugar

¼ cup (½ stick) butter, melted

3 packages (8 ounces each) cream cheese, softened

1 cup packed brown sugar

1 teaspoon ground cinnamon

½ teaspoon ground ginger

¼ teaspoon ground nutmeg

2 eggs

2 egg yolks

1 cup solid-pack pumpkin

MAKES 10 TO 12 SERVINGS

1 Preheat oven to 350°F. For crust, combine cookie crumbs, pecans, granulated sugar and butter in medium bowl; mix well. Press crumb mixture evenly in bottom of ungreased 9-inch springform pan. Bake 8 to 10 minutes or until golden brown.

2 For filling, beat cream cheese in bowl of stand mixer on medium until fluffy. Add brown sugar, cinnamon, ginger and nutmeg; beat until well blended. Beat in eggs and egg yolks, one at a time, beating well after each addition. Beat in pumpkin. Pour mixture into crust.

3 Bake 1 hour or until edges are set but center is still moist. Turn off oven; let cheesecake stand in oven with door ajar 30 minutes. Transfer to wire rack. Loosen edge of cheesecake from side of pan with thin metal spatula; cool completely in pan on wire rack. Cover; refrigerate at least 24 hours or up to 48 hours before serving.

German Chocolate Cake

• • •

½ cup hot water

4 ounces semisweet chocolate, chopped

2¼ cups all-purpose flour

1 teaspoon baking soda

½ teaspoon salt

1 cup (2 sticks) butter, softened

2 cups sugar

4 eggs

1 cup buttermilk

1 teaspoon vanilla

Coconut Pecan Frosting
(recipe follows)

MAKES 10 TO 12 SERVINGS

1 Preheat oven to 350°F. Grease and flour two 8- or 9-inch round cake pans.

2 Combine water and chocolate in double boiler over boiling water. Stir constantly until chocolate melts. Combine flour, baking soda and salt in medium bowl.

3 Beat butter and sugar in bowl of stand mixer on medium-high about 2 minutes or until fluffy. Add eggs, one at a time, beating on medium until blended after each addition. Gradually add melted chocolate on medium; beat 15 seconds or just until blended. Add flour mixture, buttermilk and vanilla on low; mix about 30 seconds or until well blended. Pour batter into prepared pans.

4 Bake 35 to 45 minutes or until toothpick inserted into centers comes out clean. Cool in pans 10 minutes. Remove to wire racks to cool completely.

5 Prepare Coconut Pecan Frosting; fill and frost top of cake.

Coconut Pecan Frosting

1 cup sugar

¾ cup evaporated milk

3 eggs, beaten

⅓ cup butter

1 cup flaked coconut

1 cup chopped pecans

1 Combine sugar, evaporated milk, eggs and butter in large saucepan. Cook and stir over medium heat until mixture begins to thicken.

2 Transfer mixture to bowl of stand mixer. Add coconut and pecans; beat on low until thick and spreadable. Refrigerate until ready to use.

KitchenAid

White Chocolate Cake

• • •

2 cups all-purpose flour

2¼ teaspoons baking powder

½ teaspoon salt

1 cup milk

½ cup (1 stick) butter

4 ounces white chocolate, broken into pieces

1½ cups sugar

4 eggs

1 teaspoon vanilla

12 ounces bittersweet chocolate, chopped

1¼ cups heavy cream

White chocolate curls (optional)

MAKES 10 TO 12 SERVINGS

1 Preheat oven to 350°F. Spray two 9-inch round cake pans with nonstick cooking spray.

2 Combine flour, baking powder and salt in medium bowl. Combine milk, butter and white chocolate in medium saucepan; cook and stir over medium-low heat until melted and smooth.

3 Beat sugar and eggs in bowl of stand mixer on medium 3 minutes or until pale and thick. Add vanilla; beat until blended. Slowly add flour mixture, beating until well blended. Slowly beat in milk mixture. Pour batter into prepared pans.

4 Bake 24 to 28 minutes or until toothpick inserted into centers comes out clean. Cool in pans 15 minutes. Remove to wire racks to cool completely.

5 Place bittersweet chocolate in medium bowl. Heat cream in small saucepan over medium-low heat until bubbles appear around edge of pan. Pour over chocolate; let stand 2 minutes. Stir until smooth. Let stand 15 minutes or until thick enough to spread.

6 Place one cake layer on serving plate; spread with one third of chocolate mixture. Top with remaining cake layer; frost top and sides of cake. Garnish with white chocolate curls.

Marble Cheesecake

• • •

1 cup graham cracker crumbs

¼ cup packed brown sugar

3 tablespoons butter, melted

4 packages (8 ounces each)
cream cheese, softened

2 teaspoons vanilla

1¾ cups granulated sugar

4 eggs

2 ounces unsweetened chocolate, melted

MAKES 10 TO 12 SERVINGS

1 Preheat oven to 325°F. For crust, combine graham cracker crumbs, brown sugar and butter in medium bowl; mix well. Press crumb mixture evenly in bottom of ungreased 9-inch springform pan.

2 Beat cream cheese, vanilla and granulated sugar in bowl of stand mixer on medium-high 2 minutes or until fluffy. Add eggs, one at a time, beating on low until blended after each addition. Beat on medium 30 seconds.

3 Pour one third of batter into small bowl. Add chocolate; mix well. Drop spoonfuls of chocolate and plain batter into prepared pan. Swirl lightly with knife.

4 Bake 1½ hours. Cool on wire rack 30 minutes. Loosen edge of cheesecake from side of pan with thin metal spatula; cool completely in pan on wire rack. Cover; refrigerate at least 2 hours before serving.

Classic **Chocolate Cake**

● ● ●

2 cups all-purpose flour

⅔ cup unsweetened cocoa powder

1¼ teaspoons baking soda

1 teaspoon salt

¼ teaspoon baking powder

1 cup granulated sugar

¾ cup (1½ sticks) butter, softened

⅔ cup packed brown sugar

3 eggs

1 teaspoon vanilla

1⅓ cups water

Chocolate Frosting
(page 260)

MAKES 10 TO 12 SERVINGS

1 Preheat oven to 350°F. Grease 13×9-inch baking pan.

2 Combine flour, cocoa, baking soda, salt and baking powder in medium bowl. Beat granulated sugar, butter and brown sugar in bowl of stand mixer on medium-high 2 minutes or until light and creamy. Add eggs and vanilla; beat 2 minutes. Add flour mixture alternately with water; beat just until blended. Pour batter into prepared pan.

3 Bake 25 to 35 minutes or until toothpick inserted into center comes out clean. Cool completely in pan on wire rack.

4 Prepare Chocolate Frosting; frost cake.

Red Velvet Cupcakes

• • •

2¼ cups all-purpose flour

1 teaspoon salt

2 bottles (1 ounce each) red food coloring

3 tablespoons unsweetened cocoa powder

1 cup buttermilk

1 teaspoon vanilla

1½ cups sugar

½ cup (1 stick) butter, softened

2 eggs

1 teaspoon white vinegar

1 teaspoon baking soda

Cream Cheese Frosting (page 270)

Toasted coconut (optional)

MAKES 18 CUPCAKES

1 Preheat oven to 350°F. Line 18 standard (2½-inch) muffin cups with paper baking cups.

2 Combine flour and salt in medium bowl. Gradually stir food coloring into cocoa in small bowl until blended and smooth. Combine buttermilk and vanilla in separate small bowl.

3 Beat sugar and butter in bowl of stand mixer on medium 4 minutes or until very light and fluffy. Add eggs, one at a time, beating well after each addition. Add cocoa mixture; beat until well blended and uniform in color. Add flour mixture alternately with buttermilk mixture, beating just until blended. Combine vinegar and baking soda in small bowl; gently fold into batter with spatula or spoon (do not use mixer). Spoon batter evenly into prepared muffin cups.

4 Bake 18 to 20 minutes or until toothpick inserted into centers comes out clean. Cool in pans on wire racks 10 minutes. Remove to wire racks to cool completely.

5 Prepare Cream Cheese Frosting; pipe or spread on cupcakes. Sprinkle with coconut, if desired.

Carrot Cake

• • •

1 cup (2 sticks) butter, melted

4 eggs

2 cups all-purpose flour

1½ cups sugar

1½ teaspoons baking powder

1 teaspoon cinnamon

¼ teaspoon salt

2½ cups finely grated carrots

½ cup chopped walnuts, plus additional for garnish

Cream Cheese Frosting (recipe follows)

MAKES 10 TO 12 SERVINGS

1 Preheat oven to 350°F. Grease and flour 9-inch springform pan.

2 Combine butter and eggs in bowl of stand mixer; beat on medium-high 1 minute. Add flour, sugar, baking powder, cinnamon and salt; mix on medium-low 30 seconds or until combined. Add carrots and ½ cup walnuts; mix on low 10 seconds. Pour batter into prepared pan.

3 Bake 1 hour 15 minutes (do not test doneness with toothpick inserted into center). Cool in pan on wire rack 10 minutes. Loosen edge of cake from side of pan with thin metal spatula; remove side and bottom. Cool completely on wire rack.

4 Prepare Cream Cheese Frosting. Split cake into two layers; fill and frost cake. Garnish with additional walnuts.

Cream Cheese Frosting

12 ounces cream cheese, softened

½ cup (1 stick) butter, softened

2 teaspoons vanilla

1½ cups powdered sugar

1 Combine cream cheese, butter and vanilla in bowl of stand mixer; beat on medium-high 2 minutes.

2 Sift powdered sugar into bowl. Beat on low 30 seconds or just until combined. Beat on medium-high 2 minutes or until well blended and fluffy. Refrigerate until ready to use.

Festive **Chocolate Cupcakes**

• • •

¾ cup all-purpose flour

½ cup unsweetened cocoa powder

1 teaspoon baking powder

½ teaspoon salt

½ cup (1 stick) butter, softened

1 cup plus 2 tablespoons granulated sugar

2 eggs

1 teaspoon vanilla

½ cup milk

6 ounces bittersweet chocolate, chopped

½ cup heavy cream

Powdered sugar

MAKES 12 CUPCAKES

1 Preheat oven to 350°F. Line 12 standard (2½-inch) muffin cups with paper baking cups.

2 Combine flour, cocoa, baking powder and salt in small bowl. Beat butter in bowl of stand mixer on medium until creamy. Add granulated sugar; beat 3 to 4 minutes. Add eggs, one at a time, beating well after each addition. Beat in vanilla. Add flour mixture alternately with milk, beginning and ending with flour mixture. Spoon batter evenly into prepared muffin cups.

3 Bake about 20 minutes or until toothpick inserted into centers comes out clean. Cool cupcakes in pans on wire racks 10 minutes. Remove to wire racks to cool completely.

4 Place bittersweet chocolate in medium bowl. Heat cream in small saucepan over medium-low heat until bubbles appear around edge of pan. Pour over chocolate; let stand 2 minutes. Stir until smooth. Dip tops of cupcakes in chocolate mixture; return to wire rack until set.

5 Place stencil gently over cupcakes; sprinkle with powdered sugar.

○ **TIP**

STENCILS CAN BE FOUND AT CRAFT STORES AND BAKING SUPPLY STORES. YOU CAN ALSO MAKE YOUR OWN STENCILS BY CUTTING OUT SHAPES FROM PAPER.

KitchenAid

Velvety Coconut Spice Cake

● ● ●

½ cup granulated sugar, plus additional for pans

2½ cups all-purpose flour

1½ teaspoons baking powder

1½ teaspoons ground cinnamon

¾ teaspoon baking soda

½ teaspoon salt

¼ teaspoon ground cloves

¼ teaspoon ground nutmeg

¼ teaspoon ground allspice

¼ teaspoon ground cardamom

1½ cups light cream

¼ cup molasses

½ cup (1 stick) butter, softened

½ cup packed brown sugar

4 eggs

1 teaspoon vanilla

1½ cups flaked coconut

Creamy Orange Frosting (recipe follows)

Candied Orange Rose (recipe follows, optional)

⅔ cup orange marmalade

MAKES 10 TO 12 SERVINGS

1 Preheat oven to 350°F. Grease three 8-inch round cake pans; sprinkle with enough granulated sugar to lightly coat bottoms and sides of pans.

2 Combine flour, baking powder, cinnamon, baking soda, salt, cloves, nutmeg, allspice and cardamom in medium bowl. Combine cream and molasses in small bowl.

3 Beat butter in bowl of stand mixer on medium until creamy. Add ½ cup granulated sugar and brown sugar; beat until light and fluffy. Add eggs, one at a time, beating well after each addition. Stir in vanilla. Add flour mixture alternately with molasses mixture, beating well on low after each addition. Stir in coconut. Pour batter evenly into prepared pans.

4 Bake 20 minutes or until toothpick inserted into centers comes out clean. Cool in pans on wire racks 10 minutes. Loosen edges; remove to racks to cool completely.

5 Prepare Creamy Orange Frosting and Candied Orange Rose, if desired.

6 Spread two cake layers with marmalade; stack on serving plate. Top with third cake layer. Frost with Creamy Orange Frosting. Refrigerate until ready to serve. Garnish with Candied Orange Rose.

Creamy Orange Frosting

3 ounces cream cheese, softened

2 cups powdered sugar

Few drops orange extract

Milk (optional)

Beat cream cheese in bowl of stand mixer on medium-high until creamy. Gradually add powdered sugar, beating until fluffy. Blend in orange extract. Add milk, 1 tablespoon at a time, until desired consistency is reached.

Candied Orange Rose

1 cup sugar

1 cup water

1 orange, thinly peeled in long strips

1 Bring sugar and water to a boil in medium saucepan over medium-high heat, stirring occasionally.

2 Roll up orange peel; secure with toothpicks. Place on slotted spoon; add to hot sugar syrup. Reduce heat to low; simmer 5 to 10 minutes or until orange rind turns translucent. Remove from syrup; cool completely. Remove toothpicks.

Berry Cupcake Shorties

• • •

1½ cups all-purpose flour

½ cup plus 2 tablespoons sugar, divided

¾ teaspoon baking powder

½ teaspoon salt

¼ teaspoon baking soda

1 cup milk

2 eggs

⅓ cup canola oil

1 teaspoon vanilla

2 tablespoons unsweetened cocoa powder

4 cups fresh strawberries, sliced

Whipped cream

MAKES 12 CUPCAKES

1 Preheat oven to 350°F. Line 12 standard (2½-inch) muffin cups with paper baking cups.

2 Combine flour, ½ cup sugar, baking powder, salt and baking soda in large bowl. Add milk, eggs, oil and vanilla; mix until well blended. Transfer half of batter to 2-cup glass measure or medium bowl; stir in cocoa until blended. Divide vanilla batter evenly among prepared muffin cups. Spoon chocolate batter evenly over vanilla batter. Swirl with knife to marbleize.

3 Bake 18 to 20 minutes or until lightly browned and toothpick inserted into centers comes out clean. Cool completely in pan on wire rack.

4 Mash about one third of strawberries in medium bowl. Stir in remaining strawberries and 2 tablespoons sugar. Cut cupcakes in half. Spoon berry mixture over cupcake bottoms; top with whipped cream and cupcake tops.

KitchenAid

Angel Food Cake

• • •

1¼ cups all-purpose flour

1½ cups sugar, divided

1½ cups egg whites
(about 12 to 15 egg whites)

1½ teaspoons cream of tartar

1½ teaspoons vanilla *or* ½ teaspoon
almond extract

¼ teaspoon salt

MAKES 10 TO 12 SERVINGS

1 Preheat oven to 375°F. Combine flour and ½ cup sugar in small bowl.

2 Place egg whites in bowl of stand mixer; attach wire whip to mixer. Gradually turn to medium-high and whip 30 seconds to 1 minute until egg whites are frothy. Add cream of tartar, vanilla and salt; whip on high 2 to 2½ minutes until whites are almost stiff but not dry.

3 Gradually add remaining 1 cup sugar on low; mix about 1 minute. Fold in one fourth of flour mixture at a time with spatula just until blended. Pour batter into ungreased 10-inch tube pan. Gently cut through batter with knife to break up large air bubbles.

4 Bake 35 minutes or until crust is golden brown and cracks are very dry. Immediately invert cake pan onto funnel or soft drink bottle. Cool completely. Remove from pan.

Easy White Cake

• • •

2 cups all-purpose flour

1½ cups sugar

3 teaspoons baking powder

½ teaspoon salt

½ cup shortening

1 cup milk

1 teaspoon vanilla

4 egg whites

Buttercream Frosting (recipe follows) or desired frosting

MAKES 2 (8- OR 9-INCH) CAKE LAYERS

1 Preheat oven to 350°F. Grease and flour 8- or 9-inch round cake pans.

2 Combine flour, sugar, baking powder and salt in bowl of stand mixer. Add shortening, milk and vanilla. Mix on low about 1 minute. Add egg whites; beat on medium-high about 1 minute or until smooth and fluffy. Pour batter into prepared pans.

3 Bake 30 to 35 minutes or until toothpick inserted in centers comes out clean. Cool in pans on wire racks 10 minutes. Remove to wire racks to cool completely.

4 Prepare Buttercream Frosting; fill and frost cake.

Buttercream Frosting

• • •

¾ cup (1½ sticks) butter, softened

2 cups powdered sugar

1½ teaspoons vanilla

MAKES FROSTING FOR 2-LAYER OR 13×9-INCH CAKE

Beat butter in bowl of stand mixer on medium-high 30 seconds or until creamy. Sift powdered sugar over butter; add vanilla. Beat on low 30 seconds. Increase speed to medium-high; beat 2 minutes or until light and fluffy.

Banana Cake

• • •

2½ cups all-purpose flour

1 tablespoon baking soda

½ teaspoon salt

1 cup granulated sugar

¾ cup packed brown sugar

½ cup (1 stick) butter, softened

2 eggs

1 teaspoon vanilla

3 ripe bananas, mashed
(about 1⅔ cups)

⅔ cup buttermilk

Chocolate Frosting (page 260)

MAKES 10 TO 12 SERVINGS

1 Preheat oven to 350°F. Grease two 8-inch round cake pans. Combine flour, baking soda and salt in medium bowl.

2 Beat granulated sugar, brown sugar and butter in bowl of stand mixer on medium until well blended. Add eggs and vanilla; beat well. Stir in bananas. Add flour mixture and buttermilk alternately to banana mixture, beating on low after each addition Pour batter into prepared pans.

3 Bake about 35 minutes or until toothpick inserted into centers comes out clean. Cool in pans on wire racks 10 minutes. Remove to wire racks to cool completely.

4 Prepare Chocolate Frosting; fill and frost cake.

pies, tarts
and cobblers

Strawberry Cream Pie

• • •

1 cup plus 1½ teaspoons
all-purpose flour, divided

¼ cup plus 1 teaspoon
sugar, divided

¼ teaspoon salt

¼ cup (½ sticks) cold butter,
cut into pieces

3 tablespoons ice water, divided

¾ teaspoon white or cider vinegar

8 ounces cream cheese

¼ cup vanilla yogurt

2 egg whites

½ teaspoon vanilla

1½ cups fresh strawberries, cut in half

¼ cup strawberry jelly

MAKES 8 SERVINGS

1 Combine 1 cup flour, 1 teaspoon sugar and salt in bowl of stand mixer; mix on low 15 seconds. Sprinkle butter over flour mixture; mix on low 30 to 45 seconds or until pea-size pieces form. Add 2 tablespoons ice water and vinegar, mixing until ingredients are moistened and dough begins to hold together. Add remaining 1 tablespoon ice water, if necessary. Pat dough into smooth ball and flatten slightly. Wrap in plastic wrap; refrigerate 15 minutes.

2 Preheat oven to 450°F. Roll out dough into 12-inch circle on lightly floured surface. Place dough in 9-inch pie plate. Bake 10 to 12 minutes or until lightly browned. Cool on wire rack. *Reduce oven temperature to 325°F.*

3 Beat cream cheese, remaining ¼ cup sugar and remaining 1½ teaspoons flour in bowl of stand mixer on medium until creamy. Beat in yogurt, egg whites and vanilla; mix well. Pour mixture into pie crust.

4 Bake 25 minutes or until set. Cool completely on wire rack. Place strawberries on top of filling. Melt jelly in small saucepan over low heat; brush over strawberries. Refrigerate 3 hours or overnight.

KitchenAid

Berry-Peachy Cobbler

• • •

4 tablespoons plus 2 teaspoons sugar, divided

¾ cup plus 2 tablespoons all-purpose flour

1¼ pounds fresh peaches, peeled and sliced *or* 1 package (16 ounces) frozen sliced peaches, thawed and drained

2 cups fresh raspberries *or* 1 package (12 ounces) frozen raspberries

1 teaspoon grated lemon peel

½ teaspoon baking powder

½ teaspoon baking soda

⅛ teaspoon salt

2 tablespoons cold butter, cut into small pieces

½ cup buttermilk

MAKES 8 SERVINGS

1 Preheat oven to 425°F. Spray eight ramekins or 11×7-inch baking dish with nonstick cooking spray; place ramekins on jelly-roll pan.

2 For filling, combine 2 tablespoons sugar and 2 tablespoons flour in large bowl. Add peaches, raspberries and lemon peel; toss to coat. Divide fruit among prepared ramekins. Bake about 15 minutes or until fruit is bubbly around edges.

3 Meanwhile for topping, combine remaining ¾ cup flour, 2 tablespoons sugar, baking powder, baking soda and salt in medium bowl. Cut in butter with pastry blender until mixture resembles coarse crumbs. Stir in buttermilk just until moistened.

4 Remove ramekins from oven; top fruit with equal dollops of topping. Sprinkle topping with remaining 2 teaspoons sugar. Bake 18 to 20 minutes or until topping is lightly browned. Serve warm.

Cherry Frangipane Tart

• • •

Perfect Pie Pastry for One-Crust Pie
(page 288)

⅔ cup slivered almonds

½ cup all-purpose flour

¼ cup powdered sugar

½ cup (1 stick) butter, softened

2 eggs

1¾ cups pitted frozen sweet cherries

MAKES 6 TO 8 SERVINGS

1 Prepare Perfect Pie Pastry. Preheat oven to 450°F. Line tart pan with pie dough; trim edges. Cover with parchment paper; fill with dried beans or pie weights. Bake 10 minutes. Carefully remove paper and weights. *Reduce oven temperature to 350°F.*

2 Combine almonds, flour and powdered sugar in food processor; process until finely ground. Add butter; pulse to blend. Add eggs, one at a time, with processor running. Pour into baked crust; smooth top. Sprinkle with cherries.

3 Bake 35 minutes or until set. Cool completely in pan on wire rack.

Lemon Cheesecake Tarts

● ● ●

¾ cup (1½ sticks) butter, slightly softened

1 cup sugar, divided

2 teaspoons grated lemon peel

3 egg yolks

1 teaspoon vanilla

2 cups all-purpose flour

¼ teaspoon salt

1 package (8 ounces) cream cheese, softened

½ cup prepared lemon curd or Lemon Curd Filing (page 290)

Lemon peel strips and fresh mint leaves (optional)

MAKES 4 DOZEN TARTS

1 Beat butter, ¾ cup sugar and grated lemon peel in bowl of stand mixer on medium 1 minute. Beat in egg yolks and vanilla until well blended. Add flour and salt; beat just until combined. Divide dough into two discs. Wrap in plastic wrap; refrigerate at least 1 hour or until firm.

2 Let dough stand at room temperature 5 minutes. Spray 48 mini (1¾-inch) muffin pan cups with nonstick cooking spray.

3 Roll out half of dough on lightly floured surface to ⅛-inch thickness. Cut out circles with 2½-inch round or fluted cookie cutter. Press circles into prepared muffin cups. Repeat with remaining dough. Refrigerate at least 30 minutes.

4 Preheat oven to 375°F. Prick bottom of each cup with fork. Bake 10 to 12 minutes or until golden brown. Cool completely in pans on wire rack.

5 For filling, beat cream cheese and remaining ¼ cup sugar in bowl of stand mixer on medium. Add lemon curd; mix on low until combined. Fill each tart shell with about 2 teaspoons filling. Cover and refrigerate at least 2 hours and up to 3 days before serving. Garnish with lemon peel strips and mint.

Raspberry Cream Pie

• • •

1⅓ cups ground pecans

2 tablespoons melted butter

¼ cup plus 1 tablespoon granulated sugar, divided

¼ teaspoon ground cinnamon

1 envelope unflavored gelatin

½ cup water

6 tablespoons powdered sugar

1 tablespoon fresh lemon juice

⅛ teaspoon salt

2 cups fresh raspberries *or* 1 bag (12 ounces) frozen raspberries, thawed

1 cup heavy cream

MAKES 8 SERVINGS

1 Preheat oven to 350°F. For crust, combine ground pecans, butter, 1 tablespoon granulated sugar and cinnamon in medium bowl. Press mixture in bottom and up side of 9-inch pie plate. Bake 5 to 7 minutes or until set and lightly browned. Cool completely.

2 Sprinkle gelatin over ½ cup water in medium saucepan; let stand about 5 minutes or until gelatin is softened. Add powdered sugar, remaining ¼ cup granulated sugar, lemon juice and salt; cook and stir over medium-low heat until sugar and gelatin are completely dissolved. Stir in raspberries. Let stand about 30 minutes or until thickened.

3 Beat cream in bowl of stand mixer on high until stiff peaks form. Fold in raspberry mixture. Gently spoon into prepared crust. Refrigerate 2 to 3 hours before serving.

Perfect Pie **Pastry**

• • •

2¼ cups all-purpose flour

¾ teaspoon salt

½ cup cold shortening, cut into pieces

2 tablespoons cold butter, cut into pieces

5 to 6 tablespoons ice water

MAKES 2 (8- OR 9-INCH) CRUSTS

1 Combine flour and salt in bowl of stand mixer; mix on low 15 seconds. Sprinkle shortening and butter over flour mixture; mix on low 30 to 45 seconds or until pea-size pieces form. Add ice water 1 tablespoon at a time on low, mixing until ingredients are moistened and dough begins to hold together. Divide dough in half. Pat each half into smooth ball and flatten slightly. Wrap in plastic wrap. Refrigerate 15 minutes.

2 Roll one half of dough to ⅛-inch thickness between sheets of waxed paper. Fold pastry into quarters. Ease into 8- or 9-inch pie plate and unfold, pressing firmly against bottom and sides.

FOR ONE-CRUST PIE: Fold edge under. Crimp as desired. Add desired pie filling. Bake as directed.

FOR TWO-CRUST PIE: Trim pastry even with edge of pie plate. Roll out second piece of dough. Add desired pie filling. Top with second piece of dough. Seal edge and crimp as desired. Cut slits for steam to escape. Bake as directed.

FOR BAKED PASTRY SHELL: Fold edge under. Crimp as desired. Prick sides and bottom with fork. Bake at 450°F for 8 to 10 minutes or until lightly browned. Cool completely on wire rack.

ALTERNATE METHOD FOR BAKED PASTRY SHELL: Fold edge under. Crimp as desired. Line shell with parchment paper or foil. Fill with pie weights or dried beans. Bake at 450°F for 10 to 12 minutes, or until edges are lightly browned. Remove pie weights and parchment paper. Cool completely on wire rack.

KitchenAid

Classic Apple Pie

• • •

Perfect Pie Pastry for Two-Crust Pie (page 288)

1 cup sugar, plus additional for garnish

2 tablespoons all-purpose flour

1 teaspoon ground cinnamon

⅛ teaspoon salt

⅛ teaspoon ground nutmeg

6 to 8 medium tart cooking apples, peeled, cored and thinly sliced

2 tablespoons butter

MAKES 8 SERVINGS

1 Prepare Perfect Pie Pastry. Preheat oven to 400°F.

2 Combine 1 cup sugar, flour, cinnamon, salt and nutmeg in large bowl. Stir in apples. Pour filling into pastry in pie plate; dot with butter. Top with second piece of pastry. Seal edge and crimp as desired. Sprinkle with additional sugar, if desired.

3 Bake 50 minutes. Cool completely on wire rack.

Lemon Curd Tart with Fresh Blueberries

● ● ●

Lemon Curd Filling (recipe follows)

4 (12×17-inch) sheets phyllo dough, thawed

²⁄₃ cup butter, melted

½ pint fresh blueberries

MAKES 6 SERVINGS

1 Prepare Lemon Curd Filling. Preheat oven to 375°F. Spray 6 standard (2½-inch) muffin pan cups with nonstick cooking spray.

2 Place one sheet of phyllo dough on work surface; cover remaining phyllo with damp cloth until ready to use. Brush phyllo with butter; place another sheet on top. Repeat with remaining phyllo and butter.

3 Cut dough into six equal squares. Fit 1 square into each cup of a well-greased muffin tin. Pleat dough to fit if necessary. Work quickly so dough does not dry out. Bake 12 to 14 minutes. Cool completely.

4 Spoon about ⅓ cup filling into each tart shell. Sprinkle with fresh blueberries. Serve immediately.

Lemon Curd Filling

¾ **cup sugar**

½ **cup plus 1 tablespoon fresh lemon juice**

Pinch of salt

6 **egg yolks**

½ **cup (1 stick) butter, softened**

1 Combine sugar, lemon juice and salt in bowl of stand mixer; attach wire whip to mixer. Whip on medium 1 minute. Increase speed to high; add egg yolks, one at a time, whipping about 30 seconds after each addition. With mixer running on high, add butter, 1 tablespoon at a time, mixing about 15 seconds after each addition. Whip 30 seconds (mixture will appear curdled).

2 Transfer mixture to medium saucepan. Cook over medium-low heat 7 to 8 minutes or until mixture is thick and smooth and just begins to bubble, stirring constantly. Do not boil.

3 Pour curd into medium bowl; press plastic wrap onto surface. Refrigerate at least 4 hours or until cold.

KitchenAid

Sweet Potato Pecan Pie

• • •

Perfect Pie Pastry for One-Crust Pie
(page 288)

1½ cups pecan halves

½ cup light corn syrup

1 egg white

2 cups puréed cooked sweet potatoes
(about 1½ pounds potatoes)

⅓ cup packed brown sugar

1 teaspoon vanilla

½ teaspoon ground cinnamon

¼ teaspoon salt

Pinch *each* ground nutmeg and ground
cloves

2 eggs, beaten

MAKES 8 SERVINGS

1 Prepare Perfect Pie Pastry. Preheat oven to 400°F. Prick bottom of pie pastry all over with fork. Bake 10 minutes or until lightly browned. Cool on wire rack. *Reduce oven temperature to 350°F.*

2 Combine pecans, corn syrup and egg white in small bowl; mix well.

3 Combine sweet potatoes, brown sugar, vanilla, cinnamon, salt, nutmeg and cloves in large bowl; mix until well blended. Stir in eggs. Spread sweet potato mixture into baked pie crust. Spoon pecan mixture evenly over top.

4 Bake 45 to 50 minutes or until filling is puffed and topping is golden. Cool completely on wire rack.

Chocolate **Pecan Pie**

• • •

Perfect Pie Pastry for One-Crust Pie
(page 288)

4 eggs

1 cup sugar

1 cup dark corn syrup

3 ounces unsweetened chocolate, melted

2 cups pecan halves

MAKES 8 SERVINGS

1 Prepare Perfect Pie Pastry. Preheat oven to 400°F. Prick bottom of pie pastry all over with fork. Bake 10 minutes or until lightly browned. Cool on wire rack. *Reduce oven temperature to 350°F.*

2 Beat eggs, sugar and corn syrup in bowl of stand mixer on medium-high speed 1 minute. Gradually beat in chocolate on medium; beat 1 minute or until well blended. Stir in pecans. Pour into pie crust.

3 Bake 35 to 45 minutes or until slightly soft in center. Cool completely on wire rack.

Deep Dish **Blueberry Pie**

• • •

Buttery Pie Dough for Two-Crust Pie
(recipe follows)

6 cups fresh blueberries
or 2 (16-ounce) packages
frozen blueberries, thawed

2 tablespoons lemon juice

1¼ cups sugar

3 tablespoons quick tapioca

¼ teaspoon ground cinnamon

1 tablespoon butter, cut into small pieces

MAKES 9 SERVINGS

1 Prepare Buttery Pie Dough. Preheat oven to 400°F.

2 Place blueberries in large bowl and sprinkle with lemon juice. Stir sugar, tapioca and cinnamon in small bowl. Gently fold sugar mixture into blueberries; mix until blended.

3 Roll out half of dough into 12-inch circle on lightly floured work surface. Fit dough into 9-inch deep-dish pie plate. Trim all but ½ inch overhang. Pour blueberry mixture into crust; dot top with butter.

4 Roll out remaining half of dough into 10-inch circle, about ¼ inch thick. Cut four or five small shapes from dough with small cookie cutter or knife. Place dough over blueberry filling. Trim dough, leaving 1-inch border around pie. Fold dough under overhang on bottom crust even with edge of pie plate. Crimp edges with fork tines.

5 Bake 15 minutes. *Reduce oven temperature to 350°F.* Bake 40 minutes or until pastry is browned. Cool on wire rack 30 minutes before serving.

Buttery Pie Dough for Two-Crust Pie

2½ **cups all-purpose flour**

1 **teaspoon salt**

1 **teaspoon sugar**

1 **cup (2 sticks) cold butter, cut into small pieces**

⅓ **cup ice water**

1 Combine flour, salt and sugar in bowl of stand mixer. Scatter butter over flour mixture; mix on low 1 minute or until coarse crumbs form.

2 Drizzle 2 tablespoons ice water over mixture; stir to blend. Repeat with remaining ice water. Squeeze dough together; turn out onto work surface. Knead dough four to five times. Gather dough into ball. Divide dough in half and shape each half into disc. Wrap each disc in plastic wrap. Refrigerate at least 1 hour.

○ **TIP**

DOUGH MAY BE
REFRIGERATED UP TO
2 DAYS OR FROZEN UP
TO 1 MONTH BEFORE
USING. IF FROZEN, THAW
IN REFRIGERATOR BEFORE
USING.

desserts

Chocolate **Crème Brûlée**

• • •

2 cups heavy cream

3 ounces semisweet or bittersweet
baking chocolate, finely chopped

3 egg yolks

¼ cup granulated sugar

2 teaspoons vanilla

3 tablespoons packed brown sugar

MAKES 4 SERVINGS

1 Preheat oven to 325°F. Heat heavy cream in medium saucepan over medium heat until bubbles begin to form around edge (do not boil). Remove pan from heat; stir in chocolate until melted and smooth. Set aside to cool slightly.

2 Beat egg yolks and granulated sugar in bowl of stand mixer on medium-high about 5 minutes or until mixture thickens and becomes pale in color. Whisk in chocolate mixture and vanilla until well blended.

3 Divide mixture among four 6-ounce custard cups or individual baking dishes. Place cups in baking pan; place pan in oven. Pour boiling water into baking pan to reach halfway up sides of custard cups. Cover pan loosely with foil.

4 Bake 30 minutes or just until edges are set. Remove cups from baking pan to wire rack to cool completely. Wrap with plastic wrap and refrigerate 4 hours or up to 3 days.

5 Preheat broiler. Spread about 2 teaspoons brown sugar evenly over each cup. Broil 3 to 4 minutes or until sugar bubbles and browns, watching carefully to prevent burning. Serve immediately.

KitchenAid

Pots de Crème au Chocolat

• • •

2 cups heavy cream

1 tablespoon sugar

4 ounces semisweet chocolate, melted

5 egg yolks

MAKES 6 SERVINGS

1 Preheat oven to 325°F. Heat cream and sugar in double boiler over boiling water, stirring constantly until sugar is dissolved. Add chocolate; stir until well blended. Remove from heat.

2 Place egg yolks in bowl of stand mixer; attach wire whip to mixer. Whip on high 1 minute. Gradually add cream mixture on low, whipping until well blended. Pour into six 6-ounce custard cups; place cups in 13×9-inch baking pan. Add 1½ inches boiling water to pan.

3 Bake 20 to 25 minutes or until firm. Refrigerate at least 2 hours before serving.

Tiramisù

• • •

6 egg yolks

1¼ cups sugar

1½ cups mascarpone cheese

1¾ cups heavy cream,
beaten to soft peaks

1¾ cups cold espresso or
strong brewed coffee

3 tablespoons brandy

3 tablespoons grappa (optional)

4 packages (3 ounces each) ladyfingers

2 tablespoons unsweetened
cocoa powder

MAKES 12 SERVINGS

1 Beat egg yolks and sugar in bowl of stand mixer on medium-high until pale yellow. Transfer mixture to top of double boiler over simmering water. Cook 10 minutes, stirring constantly. Return yolk mixture to bowl of stand mixer; add mascarpone. Beat on low until well blended and fluffy. Fold in whipped cream.

2 Combine espresso, brandy and grappa, if desired, in medium bowl. Dip 24 ladyfingers into espresso mixture, one at a time; arrange side by side in single layer in 13×9-inch baking dish. (Dip ladyfingers into mixture quickly or they will absorb too much liquid and fall apart.)

3 Spread half of mascarpone mixture evenly over ladyfinger layer. Sift 1 tablespoon cocoa over mascarpone layer. Repeat layers.

4 Refrigerate at least 4 hours or overnight before serving.

NOTE: If mascarpone cheese is unavailable, combine 1 package (8 ounces) softened cream cheese, ¼ cup sour cream and 2 tablespoons heavy cream in medium bowl. Beat with stand mixer on medium 2 minutes or until light and fluffy.

Double **Chocolate Bombe**

• • •

7 eggs. divided

1½ cups heavy cream, divided

1 envelope unflavored gelatin

1 package (12 ounces) semisweet chocolate chips

½ teaspoon salt, divided

1⅓ cups sugar, divided

1 cup all-purpose flour

⅓ cup unsweetened cocoa powder

1 teaspoon baking soda

¼ teaspoon baking powder

⅓ cup shortening

⅓ cup water

½ teaspoon vanilla

Chocolate Cut-Outs (recipe follows, optional)

2 ounces white chocolate, melted

MAKES 8 SERVINGS

1 Line 2-quart bowl with plastic wrap; spray with nonstick cooking spray.

2 Separate 5 eggs; place yolks in small bowl. Place whites in bowl of stand mixer; refrigerate until ready to use. Add ½ cup heavy cream to egg yolks; whisk until well blended. Sprinkle gelatin over mixture; let stand 5 minutes to soften.

3 Melt chocolate chips in top of double boiler over hot, not boiling, water. Stir about ½ cup melted chocolate into egg yolk mixture. Stir egg yolk mixture back into remaining chocolate. Cook until gelatin is completely dissolved, stirring constantly.

4 Add ¼ teaspoon salt to egg whites; beat on high until foamy. Gradually beat in ⅓ cup sugar until stiff peaks form. Fold chocolate mixture into egg white mixture with spatula.

5 Beat 1 cup heavy cream in clean bowl of stand mixer on high speed until soft peaks form; fold into chocolate mixture. Pour into prepared bowl. Cover and refrigerate 4 hours.

6 Meanwhile for cake, preheat oven to 375°F. Grease and flour bottom and sides of 9-inch round baking pan. Combine flour, cocoa powder, baking soda, baking powder and remaining ¼ teaspoon salt in small bowl.

7 Combine remaining 1 cup sugar and shortening in bowl of stand mixer; beat on medium until light and fluffy, scraping down sides of bowl once. Add remaining 2 eggs, water and vanilla; beat until well blended. Beat in flour mixture on medium until smooth. Pour batter into prepared pan.

8 Bake 20 to 25 minutes or until toothpick inserted into center comes out clean. Cool in pan on wire rack 10 minutes. Remove to wire rack to cool completely. Prepare Chocolate Cut-Outs, if desired.

9 Place cake on serving plate. Unmold mousse onto cake. Remove plastic wrap. Trim edges of cake around mousse, if necessary. Drizzle with melted white chocolate; refrigerate 30 minutes or until set. Garnish with White Chocolate Cut-Outs.

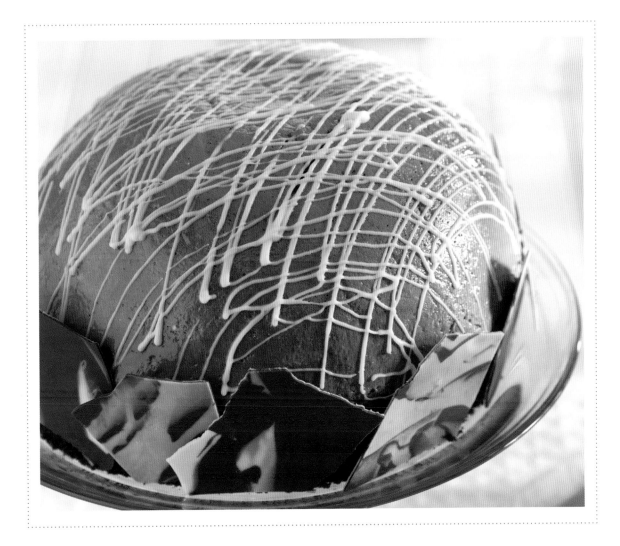

Chocolate Cut-Outs

4 **ounces bittersweet or semisweet chocolate**

4 **ounces white chocolate, coarsely chopped**

1 Line baking sheet with waxed paper. Melt chocolate in small saucepan over very low heat. Pour onto prepared baking sheet; spread into even layer.

2 Melt white chocolate in small bowl set over bowl of very hot water, stirring occasionally. Pour over chocolate layer on baking sheet; spread into even layer.

3 Refrigerate 15 minutes or until firm. Cut into large pieces with sharp knife. Refrigerate until ready to use.

French Vanilla **Ice Cream**

• • •

2½ cups half-and-half

8 egg yolks

1 cup sugar

2½ cups heavy cream

4 teaspoons vanilla

⅛ teaspoon salt

MAKES 16 SERVINGS

1 Heat half-and-half in medium saucepan over medium heat until very hot but not boiling, stirring often. Remove from heat; set aside.

2 Beat egg yolks and sugar in bowl of stand mixer on low about 1 minute or until well blended and slightly thickened. Continuing on low, very gradually add warm half-and-half; mix until blended. Return mixture to same saucepan; cook over medium heat until small bubbles form around edges and mixture is steamy, stirring constantly. Do not boil. Transfer mixture to large bowl; stir in heavy cream, vanilla and salt. Cover and chill 8 hours or until cold. Freeze in ice cream maker following manufacturer's instructions. Immediately transfer ice cream to serving dishes, or freeze in airtight container.

FRESH STRAWBERRY ICE CREAM: Combine 2 cups chopped, fresh strawberries (or other fresh fruit) and 2 to 3 teaspoons sugar, if desired, in medium bowl. Let stand while ice cream is processing. Add during last 3 to 5 minutes of freeze time. Makes 20 servings (½ cup per serving).

COOKIES AND CREAM ICE CREAM: Add 1½ cups chopped, cream-filled chocolate sandwich cookies (or other cookies, nuts or candies) during last 1 to 2 minutes of freeze time. Makes 19 servings (½ cup per serving).

KitchenAid

Orange-Scented **Panna Cotta**

• • •

2 tablespoons orange-flavored liqueur or orange juice

1 envelope unflavored gelatin

3 cups heavy cream

¼ cup powdered sugar

2 tablespoons granulated sugar

1 teaspoon freshly grated orange peel

½ teaspoon vanilla

MAKES 6 SERVINGS

1 Combine liqueur and gelatin in small bowl. Let stand 10 minutes; do not stir. (Gelatin will absorb liquid.)

2 Combine cream, powdered sugar, granulated sugar and orange peel in heavy saucepan. Bring to a simmer, stirring constantly, over medium heat. Add gelatin mixture; cook and stir 1 minute or until gelatin is dissolved. Remove from heat; stir in vanilla.

3 Spoon cream mixture into six custard cups. Let stand 30 minutes to cool. Refrigerate 3 to 4 hours.

4 Serve panna cotta in custard cups or unmold and invert onto serving plates.

Panettone **Bread Pudding**

• • •

1 tablespoon butter, softened

½ (2-pound) loaf panettone bread, cut into ¾-inch cubes

6 eggs

½ cup sugar

3 cups half-and-half

1 teaspoon vanilla

½ teaspoon cinnamon

¼ teaspoon salt

Caramel ice cream topping

MAKES 12 SERVINGS

1 Preheat oven to 350°F. Grease 11×7-inch baking dish with butter.

2 Arrange bread in dish. Combine eggs and sugar in large bowl; whisk in half-and-half, vanilla, cinnamon and salt. Pour mixture over bread; press bread down to moisten top. Let stand 15 minutes.

3 Bake 40 to 45 minutes or until puffed and golden brown. Serve warm or at room temperature. Drizzle with caramel topping.

Apple Fritters with Two Sauces

• • •

APPLE FRITTERS

Peanut oil or vegetable oil for deep frying

1 cup whole milk

¼ cup (½ stick) butter, melted

Grated peel and juice of 1 large orange

1 egg

1 teaspoon vanilla

1 large tart apple, peeled, cored and chopped

3 cups sifted all-purpose flour

½ cup granulated sugar

1 tablespoon baking powder

½ teaspoon salt

Powdered sugar

STRAWBERRY SAUCE

1 package (12 ounces) frozen unsweetened strawberries, thawed

BUTTERSCOTCH SAUCE

6 tablespoons unsalted butter

¼ cup granulated sugar

¼ cup packed dark brown sugar

⅔ cup heavy cream

1½ tablespoons lemon juice

1 teaspoon vanilla

Pinch of salt

MAKES 4 SERVINGS

1 For fritters, heat 2 to 2½ inches oil in heavy saucepan over medium-high heat until temperature reaches 350°F on deep-fry thermometer; adjust heat to maintain temperature.

2 Combine milk, butter, orange peel and juice, egg and vanilla in large bowl; beat until well blended. Stir in apple. Combine flour, granulated sugar, baking powder and salt in medium bowl; gradually stir into milk mixture until blended. (Batter will be thick.)

3 Drop batter by ¼ cupfuls into hot oil. Fry 3 to 4 fritters at a time 8 to 10 minutes, turning often, until evenly browned and crisp. Drain on paper towels.

4 For strawberry sauce, process strawberries in blender until smooth.

5 For butterscotch sauce, melt butter in small saucepan over medium-high heat. Add sugars; stir until melted. Stir in cream; simmer 2 minutes. Remove from heat; stir in lemon juice, vanilla and salt.

6 Place fritters on serving platter; dust with powdered sugar. Serve with strawberry and butterscotch sauces for dipping.

Chocolate Chili and Orange Fondue

• • •

2 (4-ounce) 60–70% bittersweet
chocolate bars, coarsely chopped

2 tablespoons butter, softened

1½ cups (12 ounces)
heavy cream

½ cup thawed frozen orange juice
concentrate,

1 teaspoon vanilla

½ teaspoon ancho
or chipotle chili powder

MAKES 6 SERVINGS

1 Place chopped chocolate and butter in medium bowl.

2 Heat cream in small saucepan over medium heat just until boiling; pour over chocolate. Add orange juice concentrate, vanilla and chili powder. Stir until chocolate is melted and mixture is smooth. Serve immediately in individual bowls or fondue pot.

Pineapple-Ginger Sherbet

• • •

2 cans (8 ounces each) crushed pineapple in juice

¾ cup sugar, divided

1 envelope unflavored gelatin

¼ cup orange juice

2 tablespoons honey

1 tablespoon grated ginger

1½ teaspoons vanilla

2 cups buttermilk

MAKES 12 SERVINGS

1 Drain one can of pineapple, reserving juice.

2 Stir together ¼ cup sugar and gelatin in small saucepan. Add reserved pineapple juice and orange juice. Cook over low heat until gelatin dissolves, stirring constantly. Remove from heat.

3 Combine drained pineapple, undrained pineapple, remaining ½ cup sugar, honey, ginger and vanilla in food processor. Cover and process until smooth. Add gelatin mixture; process until combined.

4 Stir together pineapple mixture and buttermilk in large bowl. Pour into 2- to 4-quart ice cream freezer container. Freeze according to manufacturer's instructions. Scoop into serving bowls.

Double Chocolate Mousse
with Raspberry Sauce

• • •

6 ounces bittersweet chocolate, chopped into ¾-inch chunks

6 ounces white chocolate, chopped into ¾-inch chunks

2 cups heavy cream

Raspberry Sauce (recipe follows)

MAKES 6 SERVINGS

1 Place bittersweet chocolate in microwavable bowl. Place white chocolate in separate microwavable bowl. Cover each with waxed paper. Microwave one bowl at a time on HIGH 1½ minutes; stir until smooth. Microwave at additional 30-second intervals until chocolate is melted and smooth, if necessary.

2 Heat cream in a heavy saucepan over medium heat until bubbles form around edge of pan; do not boil. Pour 1 cup cream into each bowl of melted chocolate; stir until well blended. Cover bowls and refrigerate about 2 hours.

3 Pour white chocolate mixture into bowl of stand mixer; attach wire whip. Gradually turn to medium speed and beat about 4 minutes or until soft peaks form. Spoon about ⅓ cup mixture into each of six dessert dishes.

4 Pour bittersweet chocolate mixture into clean mixer bowl. Gradually turn to medium speed and beat about 3 minutes or until soft peaks form. Spoon about ⅓ cup mixture over white chocolate layer in each dish. Cover dishes with plastic wrap; refrigerate 8 hours or overnight. Prepare Raspberry Sauce; serve with mousse.

Raspberry Sauce

1   package (14 to 16 ounces) frozen raspberries, thawed

¼   cup water

¼   cup sugar

1   tablespoon cornstarch

1 Place raspberries in blender container. Cover and blend until smooth. Pour mixture into wire mesh strainer over a small saucepan; press with back of spoon to squeeze out liquid. Discard seeds and pulp in strainer.

2 Add remaining ingredients to saucepan. Cook over medium heat, stirring constantly, until thickened and bubbly. Remove from heat and cool. Store sauce in covered container in refrigerator. Stir before using.

KitchenAid

KitchenAid

KitchenAid

KitchenAid

METRIC CONVERSION CHART

VOLUME MEASUREMENTS (dry)

$\frac{1}{8}$ teaspoon = 0.5 mL
$\frac{1}{4}$ teaspoon = 1 mL
$\frac{1}{2}$ teaspoon = 2 mL
$\frac{3}{4}$ teaspoon = 4 mL
1 teaspoon = 5 mL
1 tablespoon = 15 mL
2 tablespoons = 30 mL
$\frac{1}{4}$ cup = 60 mL
$\frac{1}{3}$ cup = 75 mL
$\frac{1}{2}$ cup = 125 mL
$\frac{2}{3}$ cup = 150 mL
$\frac{3}{4}$ cup = 175 mL
1 cup = 250 mL
2 cups = 1 pint = 500 mL
3 cups = 750 mL
4 cups = 1 quart = 1 L

VOLUME MEASUREMENTS (fluid)

1 fluid ounce (2 tablespoons) = 30 mL
4 fluid ounces ($\frac{1}{2}$ cup) = 125 mL
8 fluid ounces (1 cup) = 250 mL
12 fluid ounces ($1\frac{1}{2}$ cups) = 375 mL
16 fluid ounces (2 cups) = 500 mL

WEIGHTS (mass)

$\frac{1}{2}$ ounce = 15 g
1 ounce = 30 g
3 ounces = 90 g
4 ounces = 120 g
8 ounces = 225 g
10 ounces = 285 g
12 ounces = 360 g
16 ounces = 1 pound = 450 g

DIMENSIONS

$\frac{1}{16}$ inch = 2 mm
$\frac{1}{8}$ inch = 3 mm
$\frac{1}{4}$ inch = 6 mm
$\frac{1}{2}$ inch = 1.5 cm
$\frac{3}{4}$ inch = 2 cm
1 inch = 2.5 cm

OVEN TEMPERATURES

250°F = 120°C
275°F = 140°C
300°F = 150°C
325°F = 160°C
350°F = 180°C
375°F = 190°C
400°F = 200°C
425°F = 220°C
450°F = 230°C

BAKING PAN SIZES

Utensil	Size in Inches/Quarts	Metric Volume	Size in Centimeters
Baking or Cake Pan (square or rectangular)	8 × 8 × 2	2 L	20 × 20 × 5
	9 × 9 × 2	2.5 L	23 × 23 × 5
	12 × 8 × 2	3 L	30 × 20 × 5
	13 × 9 × 2	3.5 L	33 × 23 × 5
Loaf Pan	8 × 4 × 3	1.5 L	20 × 10 × 7
	9 × 5 × 3	2 L	23 × 13 × 7
Round Layer Cake Pan	8 × 1½	1.2 L	20 × 4
	9 × 1½	1.5 L	23 × 4
Pie Plate	8 × 1¼	750 mL	20 × 3
	9 × 1¼	1 L	23 × 3
Baking Dish or Casserole	1 quart	1 L	—
	1½ quart	1.5 L	—
	2 quart	2 L	—